To- Cookie,

Enjoy!

Loclear Mallamo

Canine Heaven

Lodean Mallamo

Seattle, Washington
Portland, Oregon
Denver, Colorado
Vancouver, B.C.
Scottsdale, Arizona
Milwaukee, Wisconsin
Minneapolis, Minnesota
Chicago, Illinois

ISBN # 0-89716-868-2
15.5089
Cover design: David Marty
Production: Elizabeth Lake

First printing August 1999
10 9 8 7 6 5 4 3 2 1

Peanut Butter Publishing
Pier 55, Suite 301 1101 Alaskan Way • Seattle, WA 98101-2982
(206) 748-0345 • FAX (206) 748-0343
Portland, OR (503) 222-5527 • Denver, CO (303) 322-0065
Vancouver, B.C. (604) 688-0320 • Scottsdale, AZ (602) 947-3575
St. Paul, MN (612) 922-3355 • Milwaukee, WI (414) 228-0800
e mail: pnutpub@aol.com
WWW home page: http://www.pbpublishing.com

Printed in United States of America

This book is dedicated
to
the wonderful world of Canines
where tails will wag ... eyes will shine
when given the chance ...

and for Missy
who loves them all.

Acknowledgements

To the former owners of some of the canines mentioned in this book, I will remember along with you as you read about them.

My thanks to Mr. and Mrs. James Ive, Mr. and Mrs. Herbert Epstein, Mr. and Mrs. Richard Parsell, Mr. and Mrs. Wolfgang Schunter, Mr. and Mrs. Howard Shulman, Mr. and Mrs. Paul Pompermayer, Bud and Sharon Johnson, Gene and Tami, and many special thanks to my friend, Beverly, who heard enough of this story to last a lifetime while it was being written.

I also thank Victor for his support and guidance to the end ... publication.

For all the joy,
Love and happiness
We bring ...
Surely, there is a
Place for us.

     Canine Heaven? Yes, CANINE HEAVEN! Oh, it is not at all like The Heaven. It is THEIR Heaven, though, —where they go when they leave Earth, and us. It is where they also built a society, and made it work! THEY?

     They are a canine population. This is their afterlife. Perhaps we humans maybe could learn from these canines a bout successful "society making". This might be possible if there was communication between the Asteroids in Canis Major's Constellation, where they are, and the Planet Earth. Well, those canines are working on that! They are a resourceful bunch, and progress is important!

     Some of the canines, when on Earth, were known to the Author. Others could have served and loved elsewhere. They all became very precious, however, as their stories came into focus, and it was found that in Canine Heaven, is a fine and intelligent community of canines. Nothing more. Nothing less.

Table of Contents

JETAWAY'S DILEMMA

There is no ill, there is no bill
That love won't pay in full.
We sing this message to you tonight-
We know your woes will come out right!

I can hear the Canine Heaven Choir singing in the Chapel. I will stop and listen for awhile before I walk to the Big Bone Palace to face His Greatness, The Great Collie. I love to sing and I join the choir when I can. But, I have lost my wings again, so I am unable to take my place beside the eleven other male sopranos. In fact, I cannot openly participate in any of the wonderful activities in Canine Heaven until this period of wing-loss is completed. Just one more week! But, I need my wings so desperately right now. And why, oh why does The Great Collie want to see me?

I have lost my wings before, but it has not mattered so much. I would take my week or two of suspension in stride and vow to do better. Sometimes a good intention just won't work. Especially when one is dealing with Napoleon.

Napoleon is a German Shepherd. Mind you, I am talking about the Constable of Canine Heaven who goes right by the book. Once he sniffs an infraction, no matter how minor, it's wing-loss time!

Now, Napoleon isn't mean. No! That would never be allowed! Not in Canine Heaven. Napoleon simply does his work too well! My mistake was far too minor for Napoleon's righteous ruling. And I do mean minor!

You see, there are five of us males who sing in the Chapel, and we are all Spaniels of one breed or another. And fun-loving and frisky. Not a bit like the other seven male soprano voices in the choir. They are all business. We are dedicated, too, but we still are a happy group. We find humor everywhere! Even in Chapel. If something is funny, we giggle. Not obtrusively, of course. I'd never do that! Not in Chapel. Only a private, eye-exchanging grin. That's all it was. But Napoleon, always ready and eager to issue a citation for most any reason, gave the two of us offenders a two-week suspension! Without our wings! And I need my wings now! Yes, I need my wings! Badly!

Like I said, these suspensions have not been a burden before, but today is a different matter. I need my wings to travel from cloud to cloud to alert my Canine Connections that a major crisis is developing on Earth. I heard of it from a news item delivered to the News Bureau of Canine Heaven by the Carrier Press Pigeon Service. Buddy, a Bloodhound, who works in the Canine Weekly Newspaper office told me about it, and said the item concerned my Connections as well as myself.

Now, my Connections, of course, are the canine inhabitants of Canine Heaven who have shared the same Master and Mistress with me at various times when on

Earth. There are four of them. The Old Black Dog, Rover, Pasha, and Buster. I do not know any of these Canines very well. Our times on Earth were far apart. The Old Black Dog, a Coonhound, and Rover, a small shaggy Terrier-mix, served together in our human family. I came along much later. Pasha followed me, and Buster was the last to come to Canine Heaven. We are still family! We have family business to attend to, and I must contact them. But how? Without my wings, I cannot go to the different communities where they reside. This is a worry! It is more than a worry! I am facing a real dilemma! And I know it!

I hoped to see either The Old Black Dog or Rover when they attended Chapel today. They never miss Chapel. But I cannot find them. I can wait for a few more minutes before I must, well, have to face The Great Collie. And I don't know why!

His Greatness does not concern himself with a mere loss of wings. He is aware of Napoleon's desire to abide by the rules of Canine Heaven, and is not likely to interfere in my wing loss. I am sure of that. It is something else! But what something else? I know I may be working myself into a state where I can't think rationally. I am worried. I am sick at heart. I can't locate any of my Connections. I can't imagine why I have been summoned to the Palace. I need to talk. Yes, I need to talk!

My name is Jetaway, cross Springer, and Cocker Spaniel, black shaggy coat, four white feet. I have been in Canine Heaven for quite a long time. This is where most of us canines go when Earth is no longer our home. It is an afterlife, and there are many of us here. I see lots and lots of canines every day that have earned their right to reside in this wondrous society. They, like me, received this great honor by serving their human family well. We do not change from our earthly being, and are the same in disposition, too. Our coming here was through good service. Not necessarily for good behavior!

The Great Collie is the head of all of Canine Heaven and its function as a society. He governs from The Big Bone Palace where he also resides. But why am I talking about Canine Heaven? I do not have the time right now. Besides, The Yearly Report from the Palace will be published in today's special issue of The Canine Weekly. It will tell all about Canine Heaven, its purpose along with its physical structure and how we relate to its entirety. I read the report every year because we are advised to keep ourselves informed. I will not be thinking much about the report this day, though. I am too worried! And why have I been summoned to the Palace?

I will hang around the Chapel for a bit longer. Maybe some of my connected family will appear. Buster, the Golden Retriever, will be singing with Rusty, Freddie, and Fresca in the quartet today so he is probably already involved with them. They are sure a fine group of singers. Very popular, too. Freddie is a pretty black Curly Retriever. She sings soprano in the quartet, and happily does their arrangements, too. Rusty is the bass singer. Like Buster, he is a Golden Retriever, but Rusty has a deep voice that any Bulldog would envy. The alto is sung by Fresca, a beautiful part Siberian Husky. She laughs as she admits that she doesn't know what else is in her make-up. Fresca is a doll! I think I already said that Buster sings tenor. I can hear them singing now!

Toot, toot, toot, toot my Golden Flute
That I play and play all day.
I can toot my message to you
Since I've been away.
To have, to hold, and point the way-
Then I will know evermore
That my flute, my Golden Flute
That I have played before.

The melody is arranged where a bass flute sounds like a horn. I am a good flute player, and I am usually the one chosen to perform with the quartet. I guess, though, since I can't take part in any activities today, Elmo, another flautist, is doing the "tooting". Elmo is a Fox Terrier, and such a braggart. That flute is sure not sounding like a horn! Maybe I'm not being fair. I try!

Elmo is also a smart aleck! I play the "Toot, Toot" number better than he can, and Freddie said so, too! I point my flute toward Sirius, and do the job with plenty of gusto! Elmo, I will be back! Have fun while you can.

Since Buster is busy in the Chapel, I can not give him the news brought by the Press Pigeon. Buster is a loner. I know that he is not close to Rover and the Old Black Dog, but he would get my message to them. I can't wait for him, though. So little time left now before I must go to The Big Bone Palace where The Great Collie waits for me. Why? I can't help but worry! And where, where is the Old Black Dog? Or Rover? Maybe inside the Chapel already, and I can't enter the Chapel today to find out for sure. And I can't ask any outsider for help either. This is family business! I must handle it myself. But how?

I did see Pasha, the puppy, come to Chapel with the other puppies. Lolita, the Director of the Puppy Compound, is a beautiful blond Afghan who is bossy, arrogant, and overly protective of the puppies. Now, Pasha can't help me with my problem. I know that. He is young, but he is family and I would feel much better if I could have just said Hi as he passed by. Lolita will not have the puppies upset before Chapel, she says. So I didn't say anything. I don't need Lolita on my case, too!

Lolita had no offspring of her own, and she is a born mother they say. It seems that Lolita wanted babies during her time on earth, but was injured in a terrible accident which left her unable to bear young. At least that's what my friend told me, but gossip gets around in Canine Heaven, too! I only know for certain that Lolita loves "her" babies and they love her. So in her bossy and arrogant way Lolita does a fine job as the Director of the Puppy Compound. We all know that we are "quite" welcome to visit the Compound and see "her little darlings" play and sing, but visitors, at all times, must be mindful of their behavior and not intimidate or arouse the puppies. Violators will be promptly expelled! You just don't mess with Lolita, and I'm not going to! Not this day anyway!

I also saw King, a Rottweiler, come to Chapel, and I wondered if words are still being exchanged between O'Casey, Editor of the Canine Weekly, and himself. O'Casey, an Irish Wolfhound, and King are always bickering about who is the stronger and best fighter. Like it matters! There is no fighting here and they both know it. Plenty of boasting, though.

King is very powerful, but smaller than O'Casey. No matter, he says, paddling O'Casey would be a breeze! King claims to be descended from the strong Rottweiler camp dogs that followed the Romans during their conquest of German held territory centuries ago. King enjoys bragging about his ancestors, and says their "careers" in the Roman Army accounts for his brawn. King says this mostly for O'Casey's benefit hoping to get O'Casey riled up.

What started all this hostility between King and O'Casey was when Editor O'Casey wrote an editorial which nearly caused King to forget the important no fighting rule in Canine Heaven. The editorial lambasted the Rottweilers as a "batch of braggarts and the breed of brawling bruisers", and King has been mad about it ever since. It was unfair of O'Casey. We all agreed with King! I think The Great Collie had a talk with O'Casey after the Rottweilers objected to the editorial. The Great Collie is, however, very democratic in his thinking, and he upholds editorial freedom. Still, O'Casey is called to task if he strays too far. But he never offers an apology.

Like King, O'Casey has a fine heritage. But he doesn't brag about it. He just thinks that we should be aware of his value without being told! O'Casey is every bit as arrogant as Lolita. He simply ignores most of us. Says he has no time for idle chatter, but he seems unusually friendly and happy today. He is greeting worshipers ever so nicely, and this is not like O'Casey at all!

I know The Yearly Report of The Big Bone Palace is to appear in the Canine Weekly today, and O'Casey would not be elated about that. This lengthy Yearly Report never makes anyone happy in the newsroom. Especially O'Casey's Bloodhound assistants who do the work. Maybe O'Casey has an important lecture or a special editorial planned, but something sure is happening to cause a big smile on O'Casey's face. His manner is so gracious today that it seems almost unreal! O'Casey is never gracious! Yet it is good to see him wax joyful for a change. O'Casey had a meeting with The Great Collie yesterday, but I wouldn't know what it was about. And I guess I don't really care much either. I have more than enough problems of my own! I can't solve any one of them. Where can I go for help? Right now, I just don't know, and I am feeling so desperate!

While waiting, worrying, and wiling away what little time I have before my meeting with The Great Collie, here is Lucy and Carolyn entering the Services quietly through a side door. They are late, but they see me and wave. I wave back and try to smile. Both are aware of my wing-loss, of course, since Lucy is my boss at the Library with Carolyn as her assistant. They know about the summons, too, but they don't know anything about the problem on Earth. It's no secret when a Canine loses his wing privileges, because Napoleon will post the names on the Chapel bulletin board every morning. Getting a summons is no private matter either. Family business and personal records are about the only concerns that are truly confidential.

I like Lucy. Everyone else seems to admire Lucy, too. She is a classy canine with fine manners and so well-read that it is a real learning opportunity to talk with Lucy. I guess it was just Lucy being Lucy that made her the good friend to us all that she is! Lucy is a Springer Spaniel with a little something else like Brand-X, she says in a laughing way. A perfect Librarian, and a perfect boss. That's Lucy!

Carolyn is my friend, too. And not a bit like Lucy, but a superior canine in her own way which is the "only" way according to Carolyn. She is a beautiful Black Labrador, and is truly ultra beautiful. Now that's a fact! If there are any doubts, though, all any canine has to do is just ask Carolyn. She can tell you right off that, yes, she is a pretty Black Labrador, and, yes, quite special, too! And furthermore, all you guys better watch out! "Them" Poodles, especially! Carolyn is no Poodle lover and makes sure that everyone knows it. Unique? Yes. A oner? Yes. Clever? Yes. Arrogant? Oh, yes! Intelligent? Way above average. Ambitious? Yes! Pretty? Absolutely, just ask Carolyn. Now this is Carolyn. Everybody's friend. Less a few Poodles, of course! Canine Heaven would not be complete without Carolyn, and we all know it. We do wonder sometimes, though, how Carolyn with such a flippant and arrogant attitude and her super ego, too, could ever earn a place in Canine Heaven. Maybe there is a lot that we don't know. We are glad she is here. Most of us anyway. Give or take a few Poodles!

Carolyn had difficulties in adjusting when she first arrived here. Many of her own making, but some she had no control over. Like when Hildegard, the snooty French Poodle, made Carolyn the object of Hildegard's displeasure only because Carolyn had no Connections already here in Canine Heaven, and since "this creature" spoke with "grammatical butchery", she must be unworthy of the honor bestowed upon her! Carolyn felt not at all welcome, and instead of going or asking for help, she stayed inside herself and suffered. It was Holy Joe, an Irish Setter, and the Chaplain of Canine Heaven, who finally was able to help Carolyn find her way. Holy Joe delved into Carolyn's past and found a treasure, a rare treasure of loyal and devoted service to not only one Master but two of them. Holy Joe saw beyond a beautiful canine with a shiny coat and the fractured speech of a flippant and arrogant street creature. Now Holy Joe is a pretty rare canine himself, and I sure would like to talk to him. Maybe he could help me sort out the problems that are overwhelming me, but Holy Joe is already inside the Chapel. I am not going to win today. And I know it!

Carolyn has finally found her niche in Canine Heaven. Already an Assistant Librarian, and well on her way "up" as she calls her consideration to become, of all things, The Most Private Secretary to The Great Collie! When told of her eligibility for the position, this pretty canine knowing full well that a Whippet usually was chosen for most of the staff positions said, "I am better than any Whippet for that job. They're not special with their thin backs, and those skinny legs, too! Their coats? I can't imagine those coats! Look at my coat. Did you ever see a coat so sleek and shiny? Huh?"

You have to like Carolyn. You can't help that! Many of the canines did not know that Carolyn deserved recognition for serving two Masters on Earth. When this was brought to The Great Collie's attention, he was not sure how Carolyn should be honored. And certainly there has been no offer of any kind made for The Most Private

Secretary position to Carolyn or anyone else. Carolyn hopes, though, that she will be chosen, and I know she has worked very hard learning how to be a secretary. She read almost every book in the Library, and made an effort to improve her diction, too. It has all worked out for Carolyn so far, but the biggest challenge is ahead. We think this will work out in her favor, too. Says she knows which way is up! I must leave now. Can't wait any longer.

Hildegard arrived for Chapel as I'm starting on my way again to the Palace where The Great Collie waits for me. I see she is slipping through an archway seldom used by Chapel goers. Hildegard is late for services today, too. There is her coat all trimmed and fluffed up with pompoms in the right places and a topknot on her head. And her nose is a mile high as usual. Hildegard, a White Poodle, claims to be descended from an ultra breed of Poodles bred in private kennels owned by Louis XVI.

Hildegard is one of the Seniors here, and we are expected to be respectful to those who reached such an old age on Earth. But truthfully, Hildegard is a big pain to most of us. She recognizes few equals, and is so snooty that when we speak to her, she will look like we are way off in left field. Just invisible! She is happy, though, when she is called upon to be in charge of something cultural, and then it is "My Paris, New York and London drawing room experiences". Some of us still don't like the way Carolyn was treated by Hildegard. But we have to tolerate her for she earned her being in Canine Heaven the same way that the rest of us did by loyal service to her Master. Hildegard means no harm. I am sure of that. But she "ain't" easy!

George, a St. Bernard, passed me as I turned the corner, nodded, but stops now to ask if I have seen the Northern Guys. That's what George calls Huskies and Malemutes. I tell him I haven't. I know that George is always bragging about how many lost mountain climbers a St. Bernard is expected to lead out of danger in one day. The Alaskan canines pay him little mind, saying that their work in the frozen tundra of the North Pole and the Arctic Circle was a great deal more challenging than in the Alps where George plied his trade. They say that George knows very little about an actual survival rescue mission. George keeps needling, though.

George nods again, and goes on past the Chapel. I guess he's not attending services today. I wish that I had been able to see Holy Joe before facing The Great Collie. I think it may have made my ordeal a bit more bearable. I don't know what to do except keep walking on toward The Big Bone Palace. And it is in sight now! Must not be early. Must not be late either. What is this about anyway? I need to see my Connections! I need to tell them about this problem on Earth! I need to talk to Holy Joe!

Now that Holy Joe is one fine Irish Setter. Intelligent, helpful, and very able as the religious leader of Canine Heaven. Holy Joe explains Canis Major, our Deity, so well that all of us know the origin and function of this important part of Canine Heaven. Since Holy Joe's arrival, the Chapel simply overflows with worshipers at each Service.

When I recall the fuss that O'Casey made in his editorials about Holy Joe having resided with "a bunch of dirty, no-good Hippies" while on Earth, I almost laugh out loud. Holy Joe has done a wonderful job, but O'Casey will do a double flip before he acknowledges it! He attends Chapel regularly, and sings in the choir sometimes, but he doesn't openly endorse Holy Joe, or compliment him either. Those two guys have a heap of respect for each other and both are tops in their Canine Heaven endeavors! Holy Joe is just more gracious!

I am walking a little faster now. I see no one. Most are in Chapel. All by myself ... worried ... overwhelmed! Can't contact my Connections ... can't let the Old Black Dog or Rover know there is a problem on Earth ... can't let them know how hard I tried ... did all I could.

I am summoned to the Palace to face The Great Collie ... don't know why ... am responsible, though ... will go and keep my appointment ... no choice anyway. But why am I summoned? For wing-loss? That would be no reason. Wing-losses happen everyday in Canine Heaven! But it has to be something ... maybe terrible ... and maybe I am being banished! Yes, I will maybe be sent to a lower cloud where I won't ever see my friends again, but I can't believe that! Maybe I am just an unworthy canine going over the edge!

I tried to think about other things ... I tried to talk ... I tried to reason with myself. That didn't work, though. I am still heavily burdened ... I see no solution. Maybe I have already said my good-byes! Maybe ... Maybe nobody cares. I care ... I care so much ... I (sob) ... do care ... (sob) ... so much. I wanted to do what I was supposed to do to take care of the family problem ... I couldn't ... I can't talk anymore ... (sob) ... (sob).

Lodean Mallamo

Well, let the historians write what they will about how I tried ... how hard I tried ... and failed! Yes, let them ... let them tell how it was when Jetaway, a (sob) failure faced His Greatness ... but ... (sob) ... I ... I just can't ...

CANINE HEAVEN'S
YEARLY REPORT

B efore leaving for Chapel, O'Casey had reminded his staff in the newsroom of the Canine Weekly that today's issue of the newspaper must include the very important Yearly Report. This lengthy annual message from Wrangler, Chief of Staff to The Great Collie, is prepared to inform the newcomers arriving since the last publication of the report. It also refreshes the memories of some of the Senior Canines who are confused at times. Wrangler, a very able Whippet, is mindful of the Seniors' needs. With his clipboard, Wrangler is always busy writing concerns and messages that the residents of Canine Heaven express before publication of The Yearly Report. He accommodates every item that he can, and this is why the report is long and wordy. Boring, very boring is what the Bloodhounds, Durkin and Buddy, say!

Durkin and Buddy are O'Casey's most important assistants, and are aware of their value in publishing the "Weekly" as they call the newspaper. Both love their jobs, and try to please O'Casey. Being Bloodhounds, Durkin and his pal, Buddy say they have a natural nose for news, and O'Casey should appreciate it more than he does. O'Casey appreciates no one individual when it comes to the excellence of the Canine Weekly. Just a collective effort, he tells them. "I never applaud myself," O'Casey is fond of saying. Durkin and Buddy smile when O'Casey makes this statement, and have a good laugh about it later. Today is Yearly Report day as O'Casey had said, over and over, before he left to go to Chapel this morning, "Get busy". Both Buddy and Durkin had prepared that report for so many years they could just about do it without the text. It never changed much from year to year. A very important document, though, they would tell themselves, and continue to gripe about this "two headed monster" called The Yearly Report. And Durkin grumbled some more as he sat down to "crank" up "this blasted linotype machine".

"Sure be glad when we get a new set up around here. Outdated, simply outdated!"

"Well, O'Casey says he is trying to get computerized equipment from Mars," Buddy said, "and The Condor Freight is having trouble getting there."

"Yeah," Durkin's paws flew over the keyboard as he talked. "I know what he says. O'Casey wants new machinery same as us. I'm just grumpy today. Its this report."

"Hey, Durk, did you see Jetaway? He just went by. Looked worried and half bawlin'. I wonder what's wrong. Durk, Jetaway was crying! I saw him!"

"Now you just relax, Buddy. Jetaway can outfret any canine here. He could be worried about that Press Pigeon release, but he is summoned today, too."

"Yeah, you're right, Durk."

"Yes, I'm right, Buddy. Now let all talk be done, please! I need quiet!"

Canine Heaven

THE YEARLY REPORT

TO: All Inhabitants of Canine Heaven
FROM: The Office of The Great Collie

Canine Heaven is a beautiful place. But you know that already. It is a lot smaller than Earth, and quite far from Earth, too. Canine Heaven is a cluster of nine spacious asteroids situated so close together that they are connected by Sky Bridges. Here, we call the complex of asteroids simply the community of Nine Clouds. I don't know the exact reasoning for this terminology, but am inclined to believe that it is because of intense thunderhead activity around the sky lines. Sometimes clouds form a low cover over the entire area causing the Sky Bridges to be closed. And this is why you need wings. More about that later. First, though, the Nine Clouds, and the individual community of each.

Cloud number one is the largest and also the most centrally positioned. It is called The Village of Canine Heaven with its wide streets and neatly mowed cloudscaping. The Big Bone Palace lies at the end of Main Street sloping down toward the shops and offices a quarter of a mile to the south. The shops and offices along the street are that part of Canine Heaven known as The Village.

The Village structures are the Mess Kitchen, the Library, the Collar Shop, the Newspaper Office, the Theater, the Museum, and the Chapel. We will cover each facility in detail a little later in this report. First, though, we will talk about The Big Bone Palace.

Most of you will not have much contact with the Palace. There may be an occasional open house affair which you attend, or you may have had a personal meeting with The Canine Council or The Great Collie himself. No matter, however, there is much more to know about this magnificent structure, its important function in Canine Heaven, and we are going to tell you who resides, and who works in The Big Bone Palace, too!

The Big Bone Palace rises on a vast sloping hillock, and you see the giant wall surrounding the Palace. That wall is constructed of polished chop bones, and the walls of the Palace itself are constructed of bleached dinosaur bones which are millions of years old. We do not know where any of these bones came from, or how they appeared only in the building of The Big Bone Palace. There are no bones anywhere else ... on any of the other Clouds. It is a mystery! And speaking of bones ...

The giant halls of the Palace are a mosaic of small transparent bones with gold designs on both the walls and the floor. Slick and shiny, and beautiful!

The Great Collie's throne, on which he seldom sits, is designed by using a choice antique selection of ebony wood and other materials from Venus. Small rattlesnake rattles inlaid in gold and silver and studded with pearls, rubies and other jewels decorate the throne's exterior. Very elegant! The centerpiece of The Big Bone Palace!

At present, Canine Heaven is headed by The Great Collie. Leadership changes every nine hundred years. We can find no record of prior leaders, or earlier populations in Canine Heaven. We have no knowledge of any matters concerning Canine Heaven before The Great Collie's reign. Maybe it did not even exist! We just don't know. But we do know that a charter was issued with The Great Collie's arrival in Canine Heaven and The Big Bone Palace was erected exclusively for his rule. And what a great monarch he is!

All of the business of Canine Heaven is conducted in The Big Bone Palace. A huge turtle shell table and dozens and dozens of file cabinets are found in a spacious meeting hall in the south end of the lower chambers. The members of the Canine Council occupy this area. A suite of offices used by the staffs of the Council is also located very close to the great hall. In the eastern part of the lower chamber stands long glass display cases filled with bones of all extinct animals, fowl and fish. Go and view this splendid collection! It will be well worth your time!

Now to continue with the Palace, we find that the western portion is a lot like the shopping malls on Earth. Maybe no wares to sell, but an open space where benches are provided for resting and conversation. Our Seniors are fond of gathering there. This area is known for its constant availability. Not so with the other wings of the lower section, however. The bone exhibits are a special case, and open only on Mondays and Tuesdays. But, as I told you, make an effort to see them!

The entrance to The Big Bone Palace is on the north side. When you enter, there sits Gretchen, a pretty Whippet receptionist, smiling and ready at all times to help you. The three sentries, all Whippets, have their office to the left of the great foyer. At the end of the foyer stands an ebony table inlaid with mother-of-pearl. On this table is the mummified Platypus whose huge beak holds The Great Canine Heaven Charter. We talked about it earlier in this report, but there is more to say.

The Charter is an important part of Canine Heaven. Technically, it is our constitution, and like such documents, the Charter is also open to much speculation and debate. There is ambiguity and there are sections in code, but an exactness in most of the Charter moves the governing process of Canine Heaven along. Its complete purpose, however, is not fully known.

There is a myth, though, telling us that a super intelligent canine from a distant galaxy will enter Canine Heaven in an unconventional manner and decode the Charter. This canine will then depart without speaking to anyone. Quite frankly, most of us do not believe any part of this myth. There are many students of history as well as cryptology in Canine Heaven, and we all are in agreement that the myth is flawed. Many of us also agree that the Charter only needs to be studied as our own desires dictate. There is no hurry. If a mystery exists in the Charter relating to its coded sections, then the keys will be found to solve them. We do not know the origin of the myth. The Great Collie discounts the myth totally!

Continuing now with the Palace, and its splendid architecture, we find the upper chambers devoted exclusively for use by The Great Collie and his staff. From the huge marble desk to the giant bejeweled throne, the office of The Great Collie is beautifully appointed. Being Chief of Staff, my office is just down the hall, and Most Private Secretary's office opens off both of our offices ... our meaning The Great Collie and me. I am Wrangler, but you know that!

A very, very important vault in the upper section of The Big Bone Palace is where the confidential file on each of you is kept. These files are only open to the individual, or if necessary, to The Great Collie himself. If any other canine knows the details of your past, present, or even your future in Canine Heaven, then the information came from you. It did not come from the Palace.

The Great Collie's private quarters cover the west wing of the upper tier. This tier meets the lower tier on this second level of The Big Bone Palace. A huge marble patio-like structure joins the two tiers. This area, the west and south wings, is almost a separate unit in the upper chambers. A garden in the south wing along with a glass enclosed observatory is also found. All of the cloud communities can be seen. Even on a "cloudy" day. Truly beautiful!

Besides the white marble staircase leading upwards from the lower section of the Palace, there are also exterior stairs serving the tower. The tower is the sleeping quarters of the staff. We are on duty and available to The Great Collie at all times. Unlike His Greatness, though, we do not take our meals at the Palace. Its the old mess kitchen for us!

Before we move on to the other service areas on cloud number one, we see that we have neglected to cover an important facility located near the Palace. This would be the Message Center. All official notices and Palace communiques are processed and delivered, or, filed and preserved at the Center. The crew of Whippets entrusted with carrying and handling these materials are a fine lot. They wear their badges very, very proudly. You may have noticed the special collars with the badges emblazoned in fiery red, and bearing an image of Mercury, the messenger of mythology. I doubt that Mercury could make a delivery any faster than our Whippet fleet!

Coming south on Main Street, we see the Museum ably directed by Claudius, an English Sheepdog. The Museum has an enormous collection of art objects and much literature pertaining to the history of canines, and their many, many, many contributions to the arts. There are paintings, sculptures and an enviable collection of antique collars. Go and visit the Museum, and learn what a creative group your ancient canine ancestors were. Get to know Claudius! He will tell you that the archives housed in the Museum, too, will not offer any conclusive information as to the origin of any of the splendid exhibits. Just enjoy them, Claudius says! As curator of the Museum, Claudius has fine qualifications. He was a member of a special kennel in Queen Victoria's England that guarded the royal jewels. Yes, go and meet Claudius! You will like him!

Directly across the street from the Museum is the Theater. Plays, operas, recitals, readings, lectures and musicals are presented at the Theater each week. If you like to act, or if there is a hidden desire to try it, then, by all means, go see Francine, a beautiful Samoyed, or Frothingham, a black and tan Manchester Terrier. They share the title of Director of the Theater.

Both Francine and Frothingham are a very real asset to Canine Heaven. They have performed in circuses, revues and motion pictures while on Earth and now we can enjoy them here! With his stylish air, Frothingham is a matinee idol with all the accolades that his acting bring. His version of Hamlet in Shakespeare's drama is as superb as that of Francine's Ophelia is magnificent! Get to know these talented canines, and do get involved! A little "ham" is in all of us. Right? So go for it!

No structure is close to another in Canine Heaven Village. Plenty of space to walk around, through or in between. Therefore, quite a distance beyond the Museum and Theater is the Library. You will find everything here that a first class Library offers its readers, pundits and browsers. You will find Lucy here, too! Lucy, a classy and intelligent Springer Spaniel, is the Director of the Library. Lucy's Mistress served as Chief Librarian at Oxford University, and Lucy was always by her side. I know you will find Lucy ready and able to assist you in any of your needs and interests having to do with libraries. Get to know Lucy and her staff. Read a book. Read papers or magazines. But do read!

Around the corner on Kitty Cat Lane is the Collar Shop. And no, I will not say how come there is a street by that name in Canine Heaven. I do not know! The Collar Shop is where you have your collars made. Boston, an English Bulldog, is a fine artisan with pride when he "turns" out a collar. Boston works equally well whether using metal, rope or leather, and he has even used linen and braided silk to fashion a creation of beauty. Boston's Master worked in a leather goods shop in the Old West. He made gun holsters, wide belts, jackets and coats, chaps and boots, and Boston "helped" with it all! How do you order a collar from Boston? Or anklets? Or a pair of cuffs? Well, let's talk about that.

First, if you were wearing a collar or other accessories when you became a resident of Canine Heaven, those items remain your personal possessions. But you may order additional items through the Collar Shop, and this is how. Each canine has an automatic account at the facility, and one point is added every month. The points accumulate. You may use your points any way you choose for any items you choose. Remember, and it is important that you do, that certain merchandise is more valuable than most of us normally wear. So when you order an item at the Collar Shop, be mindful of the points in your account. Boston keeps careful records, and is happy to assist you in your wants if your point account is sufficient. A plain leather collar will "cost" five or six points. Ornate collars will be more, and items with jewels or precious metals carry a very high point count. Use your points wisely!

The Newspaper Office is located on Main Street not too far from Chop-Chop Lane where the Mess Kitchen serves the "appetites" of Canine Heaven. Alright, I will tell you about the Mess Kitchen first! It's yum, yum yummy, too!

The Mess Kitchen is under the guidance of Hiro, a Chow Chow, whose human family operated several Chinese eating rooms. Hiro is well qualified in other cuisine, too. He especially likes preparing French and German dishes, and I can tell you right off, that you won't complain about the Mess Kitchen. There are some rules, though. You will take your meals at your appointed time, and there will be no disruption in the eat and conversation area. Some of you can get into lively discussions at times.

Canine Heaven

Hiro and his crew delivers meals to the Senior Community once daily and to the Puppy Compound twice each day. Lolita, the pretty Afghan Director of the Puppy Compound, will tolerate no delay in the delivery of the puppies' meals. Hiro says that absolute promptness may not always be possible. Lolita says it is possible, and highly expected. Hiro takes this comment in stride, and goes about his business. He is a great guy! Likes Charlie Chan movies, too.

Now back to the Newspaper office. I know that you will find the Editor and Chief of the Canine Weekly, O'Casey, a most interesting canine. We all do and I say that with the greatest respect.

O'Casey is an Irish Wolfhound, and a fine journalist. His Master was both a print and radio newsman, and his pride and joy, O'Casey, sat on his lap while he delivered the news. O'Casey learned his trade well. He is also a lecturer, and you may want to attend some of his excellent speeches. O'Casey deals in a variety of subjects. Make an effort!

The Chapel is at the far end of the Main Street in Canine Heaven. Its fine leader is Holy Joe, an Irish Setter. I can't begin to tell you how much goodness that Holy Joe has brought to this wonderful place we call Canine Heaven. But you know that already. Holy Joe is there when you need him. Always! Since becoming the Chaplain, Holy Joe serves well and faithfully the duties of this very important position. Go to Chapel! Services are held twice weekly, and on Wednesday evenings, too. I want to say something else about Holy Joe that you probably don't know.

Holy Joe was raised in a Commune of young men with many interests. His education, while strange to some, was an enormous learning in philosophy, religion and science. He was a quick study then, and still loves to learn. By the way, Holy Joe is the name given to him by the young men in the Commune. He is one fine canine. Get to know him!

The Canine Recreation Center, under the able direction of Racer, is across Skybridge Ten just inside Fleecy Park. This would be Cloud number two. Racer, a Greyhound, is ideal to head both the park and the center. While on Earth he was a track canine, racing and chasing the mechanical rabbit. Racer says that he was not happy doing this, and still thinks about the cruelty of the sport. Having no choice at the time, he found learning, however. "Mostly what not to do," Racer said to me once. He did get a new Master, though, and retired with the Master, a Forest Ranger. Together, always together, they tended the trees and kept the waters of the forest free from abuse. They made the parks a safe and secure place where both animal and man could enjoy their labors. Racer is so efficient in directing Fleecy Park, and its activities that we take it for granted sometimes. Appreciate, and get to know Racer better! You will be the winner! Fleecy Park's activities? Many events. Here are a few of them.

Racer arranges programs for most of the Cloud Communities. The only one he probably does not accommodate would, to no one's surprise, be the Puppy Community. The puppies do play in the park, but under the direction of Lolita. The Senior Canines enjoy watching the ball games and swimming meets. Fleecy Park does not have a swimming pool yet, but the round and very clean pond situated near the Recreation Center is used for these events. Kite flying and frisbes, canoeing and high jumping are provided along with the popular races. The race meets, held each Friday, are scheduled where similar canines compete. Often a challenge results in a larger breed or a smaller breed daring the other to an important test of ability. These races bring huge crowds to the pond to cheer their favorite. It's all good fun!

The Recreation Center, in addition to the usual games and other trappings found in such a facility, also has one small area devoted to music. Gertrude, a talented Beagle, will assist in your musical interests. There are many different instruments available, and Gertrude is proficient in all of them. It will come as no surprise to learn that Gertrude's Master was a music teacher!

You probably know Gertrude already. If you attend Chapel, then you know it is she who plays the organ so beautifully at the services. Stop by the center to talk with Gertrude about learning more having to do with the joys of music. I think perhaps you might want to play a musical instrument if you don't do so already. Who knows? Look into it!

Cloud number three is the Farm. All of our food supply comes from here. We are proud of this fine operation which is headed by Reuben, a Great Pyrenees. Reuben worked the fields and orchards, vineyards and berry patches in France, and later in California so he knows an unproductive undertaking when it comes to agriculture. Reuben's farm is something! Truly something! Here in Canine Heaven, we do not eat meat, and depend solely on the Farm as I told you. When the fruits and vegetables are ready to be processed, then the true harvest is accomplished. The drying frames, grist mills, preserving and storing jars and trays go into operation. Something is always growing at the Farm.

Now I am not going to tell you that you should visit the Farm and find out what goes on there. This is because of a requirement that all canines spend a week every two months working there. I know you will meet Reuben! All in good time! The only exemptions are the Seniors, the Puppies and the Services Directors, so whatever your regular job, your supervisor must release you for a week of farm duty when your name is on the schedule. Sometimes even The Great Collie can be seen pulling carrots and peanuts, or maybe stirring corn syrup. The Farm is a satisfying operation for everyone. We don't complain! Not often anyway, and you won't either!

Skybridge Seven connects Cloud number four with the extreme south end of Cloud number one. The Senior Community is Cloud number four exclusively. Our Senior Canines enjoy a peaceful afterlife where they have delightful events and memories to share with each other. The wisdom and experience of the older residents of Canine Heaven is very rewarding to their many visitors. Every one of them has a different way of recounting his days on Earth. The Senior Community is like a giant velvet lined jewelry box of precious gems. We lend a paw to help if needed, and we listen to our Seniors, too. Visit them often, and remember, here in Canine Heaven we defer to the Seniors in every instance and circumstance. Enjoy them!

The Puppy Community is located east of the Senior Community joined by Skybridge Six. The beautiful Afghan Hound Director of the Puppy Community is Lolita. Lolita is ultra able in this position, and everyone agrees, too! She is a positive influence as the head of an interesting part of Canine Heaven. The Puppies adore Lolita. The devotion is mutual. Yes! Yes! Much love there.

Now the Puppy Community is a lovely place to visit. Simply delightful. But before you cross that skybridge or fly to the Compound, you must first obtain permission from Lolita. She *will* welcome visitors, but has very basic, and very strict rules for this privilege.

By all means, though, visit Lolita, and see for yourself the fine job that she does in directing the Puppy Community. Just adhere to the rules and you will enjoy the experience. Good luck!

Clouds number six, seven, eight and nine are the residential, maintenance, processing and Toy Canine centers. You are already familiar with these areas, but I will touch on each one briefly.

Clouds six and seven contain sleeping and general residential quartering where each of you is assigned your own private cubicle complete with comfortable bed and chair. There is also room for a table and chest. A Day Room provides games, rest areas and snacks between meals. Your main meal is taken at the Mess Kitchen, however.

Cloud number eight is the domain of King, a Rottweiler. King is the Director of Maintenance in Canine Heaven. I know that you have noticed the beautifully kept streets, structures, parks, walks and skybridges. Well, the credit goes to King and his able crew. Have a talk with King! You will like him!

Cloud number nine accommodates both the Processing Center and the smallest canines, or Toys as we call them. They say it is more comfortable being apart from the larger canines. Their Community is adjusted to their needs, and it is a lively and interesting place! You will enjoy meeting Poncho, a Chihuahua of many talents. Poncho is the elected leader of the "Toys". Their collective breeds are very democratic with their elections and politics. A fine bunch!

The Processing Center is located in the northwest corner of the Toy Community. It is a small structure where, and you remember this, you first found out what was expected of you in Canine Heaven, and what you could expect from it, too. You were fitted for wings and assigned your quarters. You were also interviewed and tested for job preference. We all have a responsibility for making Canine Heaven work. And it does work for everyone of us here! You are given plenty of time, when you arrive, to acquaint yourself with your wonderful new home. You may choose to mingle with your fellow canines, or visit the Cloud Communities before assuming your duties as a citizen of Canine Heaven. Either way that you decide is alright!

We have covered the Nine Cloud Complex for you, but there are a few more items of information that you need for a full understanding of Canine Heaven.

The first item of interest concerns the many different breeds of us residing here. There are no provisions of a special nature for any particular resident of Canine Heaven. Your breed or pedigree may make for lively conversation with your fellow canines, and you may boast, but it means nothing at all officially! We don't care! We are all equal in Canine Heaven.

Secondly, we use Earth's calendar for months, weeks and days. We do not use the century year, however, and you will see how this works at the end of this report. The reigning year of The Great Collie's reign marks the time in the yearly cycle. It's all similar. No real confusion! No big surprise either is that we also use Earth's time clock.

The third item to remember is that we are a society, and much of our cultural structure is patterned like that of Earth. This is because our previous experiences took place there, and also because The Great Charter decrees that Canine Heaven "shall" operate thusly!

There are differences, however, and these variations are likewise in keeping with the dictates of The Great Canine Heaven Charter. One difference is that there is no sickness or disease. There is no reproduction. There is no further aging or growth. You arrived in Canine Heaven exactly as you were when you left Earth. If you were missing a limb, eye, ear or other body part, you are also missing them here. Your disposition does not change either, but a modification in behavior might be necessary in order to more appreciate the love and good will that we enjoy here.

Another important item that we want to mention is about your memory of the time spent on Earth. There is a permanent erasure of your memory for a four month period prior to your leaving the Earth and your arrival in Canine Heaven. All other memory is intact. Therefore, knowledge of this nature can not be necessary for your happiness, well-being and appreciation of Canine Heaven. This reasoning and stipulation is in accordance with The Great Charter. We do not question the wisdom or basic laws of The Great Charter, our Constitution of Canine Heaven! Remember?

There is something that you should also keep in mind, and this is the injustice which you may feel at one time or another. If you have the feeling of being treated unfairly then you should talk to Napoleon, the German Shepherd Constable of Canine Heaven. He will be able to resolve many small grievances, but a larger wrong or sadness will be referred to The Great Collie either by me or Napoleon. Or you may request an audience with His Greatness yourself.

The Great Collie is available for a hearing of reasonable concerns, but an audience request for frivolous matters will be denied. For example, some Terriers raised a fuss with Racer at the Recreation Center about having a group of felines available for an event that the Terriers called an old-fashioned cat chase. Since no species but *familiaris* is possible in Canine Heaven, or should be, the request of the Terriers was denied as a frivolity. And it was!

There are times when The Great Collie might issue a summons for your appearance at the Big Bone Palace. These summons are always private in nature, and must be attended as scheduled.

The one last item in this briefing is to remind you again of the great and special honor bestowed upon you. Serving and service is what it was all about! You served and you earned an excellent and everlasting reward. We are a family! As a family, we welcome you, our brothers and sisters. We hope that you will be happy in your after-life. I KNOW you will be! In case I am wrong, though, you do have an option.

There is an important provision in the Great Charter that provides for an immediate departure from Canine Heaven if a canine so desires. The canine may petition for his release, and he will leave Canine Heaven on the back of the Big White Eagle that brought him here.

The destination is not known. However, this does not mean anything necessarily fearsome. Probably a society of canines in a different cloud community, and maybe a different galaxy. We just do not know! No request has ever been recorded of a canine's desire for transfer from Canine Heaven!

PEACE AND GOOD WILL TO YOU

This special report was prepared by Wrangler, Chief of Staff, and serving at the pleasure of His Greatness, The Great Collie.

This 23rd day of March in the 127th year of his reign.

....

"Well," said Durkin, "that spiel is finished for another year. Thought I'd never get done. Wrangler don't want to leave anything out of his reports, but he sure can be one long-winded dude."

"Yeah," Buddy chuckled, "I know you are happy that O'Casey is doing, or at least he said he would do his editorial himself. He's got it locked in his office with some papers from the Palace. Big secret. Did you know that, Durk?"

"I saw him with something yesterday when he came back from the Palace, but I don't know what it was. O'Casey was summoned, you know, and he was walking on air afterwards." Durkin said. "Sure is nice to see O'Casey in a good frame of mind for a change."

"Don't I know it!"

"Well, O'Casey is a strange one. We all wonder what kind of Master he had. Who he served so well to earn the honor of Canine Heaven, you know. To tell you the truth, Buddy, I'm surprised to find him here."

Buddy was getting the presses ready to "roll" The Yearly Report along with the usual news, and he continued talking. Buddy's constant chatter while he worked was an irritation to Durkin who was pounding the keyboard again. Being polite, though, and talkative himself, Durkin listened to Buddy's opinions of O'Casey. After all, Durkin had started the conversation! So he let Buddy talk without being grumpy.

"I wonder sometimes what Master you served, Durk? You never told me."

"An old lady who drove a '25 Chevy, made lots of pies. Good and kind but a little loony, too. What about yours?"

"Oh, he was a cop." Buddy answered, "Didn't know much. If anybody needed a friend to serve them, he sure did. How he ever would have made it without me, I'll never know. Like you, Durkin, I'd like to know more about O'Casey's time on Earth. Think I will ask him."

"He won't tell you a thing," Durkin told Buddy, "O'Casey never talks about himself. Bet he's got secrets, though, and a lot of them!"

The two Bloodhounds continued their work. And their gabbing, too!

....

And yes, O'Casey did have a secret. In fact, he had a lot of secrets. One in particular!

O'CASEY

While Jetaway was sadly walking his long walk to The Big Bone Palace, necessary arrangements for his visit were already completed by Wrangler. Wrangler had placed Jetaway's file, and the files of Jetaway's connected family on The Great Collie's desk. Wrangler and The Great Collie did not know of Jetaway's dilemma, or the anguish that was consuming him because of it. Had they known, a messenger would have been immediately sent to aid Jetaway, and escort him to the Palace, too! Unaware, though, Wrangler worked in his office, and waited for Jetaway to arrive.

Having finished the pressing duties at his desk, Wrangler now began refiling the folders of the canines who had been summoned and dismissed earlier in the week. Scanning the files, his eye fell on the one belonging to the Irish Wolfhound, O'Casey, Editor of The Canine Weekly. O'Casey had had a special meeting with His Greatness the day before, and Wrangler did not know any of the details. O'Casey's visit, as well as all such meetings, was confidential and private.

Wrangler wondered what secrets were tucked inside O'Casey's file. Wrangler would never browse through the file of any canine unless requested. He would never betray the trust of his position in the service of His

Greatness. When his presence at confidential summonses was required, Wrangler was there. Clip board in paw as usual. He had not been present, though, when O'Casey had come to the Palace yesterday in response to a special summons. And as Wrangler returned O'Casey's folder to its proper filing cabinet, he was still wondering about O'Casey, and he didn't know why.

Wrangler actually knew very little having to do with O'Casey and his time on Earth. This canine seldom talked about himself. But Wrangler knew enough to wonder how it came to be that someone like O'Casey could earn a place in Canine Heaven. Of course, Wrangler was aware that this great privilege had to be earned by serving an Earthly master well. Wrangler could not bring himself to imagine O'Casey serving anything or anyone well. But, Wrangler reasoned, a canine had to serve to be here in this wonderful place. So O'Casey had been a serving canine, No doubt about that!

Wrangler checked to see if Jetaway had arrived. He had not. Wrangler returned to his thoughts. That O'Casey! That intelligent, assured and arrogant O'Casey! Wrangler shook his head!

In truth, O'Casey was an enigma in Canine Heaven to almost everyone. Very respected, but disliked, too. And so ...

It was the luck of the Irish on the day that brought the cuddly Irish Wolf hound puppy to the office of the Mayor of a village in County Cork. The pick of the litter was the only pay sought by His Honor for the services of Willy Boy. Willy Boy's services were much in demand for he had a fine pedigree, and when mated with other

Irish Wolfhounds of excellent pedigrees, always produced a fine litter. And the Mayor's new dog was as fine as they come! He was named O'Casey. A pampered favorite from the beginning. Willy Boy was business! But O'Casey was pleasure! Pure Pleasure!

The Mayor, having no family, gave a nod to O'Casey's playfulness and space around City Hall. The offices were his to frolic in, and the employees of the city were his playmates. The Mayor was no longer lonely, and he enjoyed "this great little guy" so much that even if it meant a "fixing" for O'Casey, there would not be another Willy Boy. So off to the Vet went O'Casey!

O'Casey practically grew up in City Hall, and went with the Mayor, who was also a radio newsman as well as a news reporter for the local print media. IT IS COUNTY CORK was the journal where a young O'Casey sat on his Master's lap; chewing on the pencils and pushing the writing pads to the floor. O'Casey sat beside the microphone while his Master reported the evening news on the radio. It was a good life! This playful sport had to end, however. O'Casey was growing. Fast!

The city offices, the radio station and the newsroom could no longer adapt to O'Casey's presence. He was a hazard in the work areas with his huge frame; his wagging tail now even with a desktop; and brawniness in general was too distracting for the employees. Kind of dangerous as well, they told O'Casey's Master.

"His tail is like a weapon," one of the secretaries said. "O'Casey's tail, when wagging, cracks like a whip, Your Honor, and I have the lash marks on my legs and back to prove it!"

The employees loved O'Casey. After all, he had been a plaything and a lot of joy as they watched him grow. Growing was the problem now, and it had to be dealt with! O'Casey's Master understood, and sadly made a decision.

The Mayor owned a sheep ranch where O'Casey would be sent for the summers. He would return to the city each fall, and reside with his Master on his huge urban estate. Willy Boy would rest for awhile at the ranch and be there until O'Casey adjusted to his new, but part-time home. The Mayor would visit often and O'Casey could romp in the big yard surrounding the main house occupied by the Ranch Overseer and his wife. Willy Boy would be in a kennel nearby. So it was settled!

O'Casey and Willy Boy left the city very early in the spring. Since Willy Boy had to remain in his kennel at all times to avoid an undesirable liaison, O'Casey was lonely. Even when he went inside the kennel to play, it was just no fun. Willy Boy ignored him. And the Collies working with the sheepherders paid him no mind as he watched through the fence. The Collies, well trained, had their duties and no time for a sad looking nonworking Irish Wolfhound, a stranger at that! O'Casey turned away, and through an open gate wandered into the Caretaker's yard.

O'Banion was the caretaker who also worked with the herders. He lived in a small cottage not far from the grounds where the main house stood. The yards of both places were separated by a low chain link fence. O'Casey could easily have jumped over the fence, but he had no reason to be interested in O'Banion or his cottage. This day, though, the open gate was inviting. Something new to explore in his loneliness.

O'Banion lived alone except for his female Dalmatian, Lady. Lady, no doubt lost or abandoned, had taken the place to be her home. She was hardly mature, and like O'Casey, still had an urge to be a playful puppy. O'Banion threw her a crust of bread or a bone when it was convenient. Otherwise, Lady was on her own, but she managed. She slipped over the fence and ate with the Collies.

Wilber, the young man in charge of feeding the Collies and cleaning their kennels, made Lady welcome. He enjoyed her, and wondered if O'Banion was mean to Lady. Wilber knew that O'Banion was mean to the Collies, and impatient and curt with the herders. The men did not complain; they had families and needed the work. The Overseer was too busy to notice their discontent. Wilber didn't like O'Banion. O'Casey liked him even less! O'Banion had cursed him when he only stood near the fence watching the grazing sheep and the Collies working with them. O'Casey concluded that this O'Banion man was simply mean! It would be a while, though, before O'Casey was to know the full measure of O'Banion's meanness and outright cruelty.

O'Casey wasn't thinking of O'Banion on this sunny afternoon when he walked into the caretaker's yard. His eye was on Lady who was rolling and playing in the grass alone. O'Casey had never seen Lady before. He was surprised and overjoyed to find another playful dog like himself, and quickly joined in the fun. They frolicked and chased; having a fine time all afternoon until O'Banion came home. He chased O'Casey away.

"Git outta here hound dog! You may be somethin' to your dumb owner, or to that stud, Willy Boy, but here you are nothin'. So git!"

Every day, however, for many weeks, when O'Banion rode off, O'Casey ran to play with Lady. He had found a playful companion, and was lonely no more. He looked forward to each dawn with great anticipation. O'Casey was happier than at any time since coming to the ranch. Sadly, his joy came to an end.

One morning Lady did not run to her friend to play, and seemed irritated a lot by O'Casey's presence. He tried to chase her and get her to chase him. It was no use, though. Lady only growled and snapped. O'Casey was puzzled as he trotted back to his own yard. What was wrong with Lady? He did not understand this behavior at all, but O'Banion did and did something about it!

When O'Banion arrived home, he knew right away what Lady's problem was. He thought that maybe he had found a way to make money. Hey, crossbreeds would sell if the father was the most famous stud in all of Ireland. Most expensive stud in all of Ireland, too! Wouldn't cost O'Banion a cent! O'Banion opened the gate to Willy Boy's kennel. It was only a minute or two before Lady walked in.

O'Casey was still puzzled. He would not enter O'Banion's yard, but watched Lady across the fence. She paid him no mind. Since Willy Boy had gone back to the city, O'Casey was more lonely than ever. Now he had no one except Wilber. And Wilber had his ranch duties, so he spent little time with O' Casey, and the Overseer's wife was too busy to bother other than give him his meals. He kept watching Lady, though, hoping that she would give him a sign in some way that she wanted to play. There was nothing!

One morning some strange happenings brought O'Casey closer to the fence of O'Banion's yard. On the night before, Lady had delivered five puppies. This was only puzzling to O'Casey for a few seconds. He was young; less than eight months old, but he knew and he grieved for Lady. She was still a puppy, too.

O'Casey watched while Lady, so much in pain, tried to care for her babies. She could hardly move, and the puppies with the Irish Wolfhound features were large, but clearly weak. O'Casey could not blame Willy Boy, and he could not blame Lady. This was nature at work. A mean spirited and tragic act of nature that should not have happened. O'Casey knew this, and he knew now who was to blame. O'Banion did this terrible deed! And he must be punished. But how? Here was evil! Here was suffering, and here was O'Casey grieving and helpless! He could not look at Lady any longer trying to do her instinctive duty. It was just too much for O'Casey, and he left to lie in the shade and think. Think!

Several days after her ordeal, Lady disappeared, and one by one the litter of puppies disappeared until there was only one left. O'Banion apparently decided to keep this healthy little male dog to sell when he was older. He gave the puppy milk in a bottle, and called him Little Ben. Little Ben had no look of anything in his make-up but that of an Irish Wolfhound. He was truly the pick of the litter! O'Casey saw it for what it was, but he loved Little Ben.

Watching the puppy growing into the fine specimen that O'Casey himself was made O'Banion chuckle with glee. This crossbreed would sell! O'Banion even encouraged O'Casey to once again enter his yard. This behavior, O'Casey could not understand, but he went to play in the grassy yard every day. Little Ben climbed all over O'Casey, and O'Casey, in his new found joy, gently rolled in the grass and froliced with the little bundle of energy. It was great fun!

O'Casey again looked forward to the warm summer mornings and another playful and enjoyable day. It reminded him of his good times with Lady before she had growled and snapped at him. Such a terrible memory! O'Casey was still sad when he thought about Lady, and he was sad when he thought about Little Ben's four siblings. He was helpless to know or to do anything about the mystery of their disappearance. O'Casey could enjoy, though, what was left of a beautiful friendship. And what was left was Little Ben, and O'Casey loved him!

O'Banion's friendly behavior still troubled O'Casey. This was an evil man, and O'Casey did not trust him. The inspection of the ranch made by the Mayor himself would take place soon. His Honor did this chore once each year. A vigorous, complete assessment of ranch activities and facilities which would also include the Caretaker's quarters.

O'Casey hoped that his Master might observe Little Ben playing in the yard of O'Banion's cottage, and suspect the truth. O'Casey's mistrust of O'Banion was growing. And he did not know why. Maybe it was because O'Banion was taking even more interest in the development of Little Ben. O'Casey was an intelligent canine, but he couldn't know O'Banion's mind. He only knew that it was an evil mind! O'Casey wished that his Master would soon visit the ranch. But the planned inspection was still a full week away!

One morning, a few days before the Mayor's expected arrival, O'Casey went to play with Little Ben as usual. But no Little Ben ran to greet him! After looking around and not finding where a puppy might be hiding, O'Casey hurried to O'Banion's door whining and pawing.

"Git outta here, hound dog!" yelled O'Banion from inside the cottage. "You don't need to look for Little Ben. He ain't here! And he won't be here! Just no use lookin' around. No SIR! So git, and don't come back!"

O'Casey eyed O'Banion who had come out of his house, and was now standing on its low porch. O'Casey was scared, and angry, too. Where was Little Ben? What had happened to him? O'Casey, now fully grown, with his huge frame trembling and his heart breaking, couldn't seem to take his leave. He kept watching O'Banion who was saying, "Now your buddy ain't here no more, so run along outta my way, hound dog! Or maybe you'd like for me to roll and frolic in the grass with you!"

"No!" thought O'Casey as he turned to leave, "I don't want to roll in the grass with you. Not today! And not tomorrow either! But I can promise there will be a roll in the grass! Just you and me! There will be a roll! WILL be a roll in the grass!"

O'Casey trotted into his own yard. He couldn't imagine pain greater than what he was feeling, but there was also anger. A lot of it! O'Banion would pay for his evil deed; whatever it was and he would pay dearly! A roll in the grass? Yes! A roll in the grass!

Winter was coming and O'Casey would be going back to the city soon. So it was in the late fall, and just a month after Little Ben's disappearance, that O'Banion was found badly wounded. Some workers said it happened when O'Banion walked alone in the fields, and that a wild boar must have attacked him. The Caretaker could not identify the force in the darkness which brought him down with such ferocity. O'Casey was never suspected. At least by the ranchers!

Shortly after O'Banion's "accident" on the range, and while he was still a patient in partial recovery, the Mayor took O'Casey back to the city. O'Casey was happy to leave behind the long and sad summer, and actually enjoyed being with his friends in City Hall again. A pleasant winter it was, but the spring came and O'Casey found himself back at the ranch.

O'Banion's former cottage was occupied by a newly hired caretaker. A decent sort of guy with whom O'Casey got along very well. The summer went along very well, too. So different from the heartache of a year ago, but O'Casey's memories, both happy and sad, would be with him for all of his life.

O'Casey did encounter O'Banion now and then during the summer. Even with his disabilities, O'Banion remained at the ranch helping out where he could. When he ran into O'Banion, O'Casey always wagged his huge tail in greeting, and thought what a roll, a hurtful and sad roll in the grass it had been. It had been necessary, though! O'Banion's own thoughts, however, ran in another direction, and he voiced them one day to O'Casey when they were alone.

"I know it was you, O'Casey! I know I can't prove it, but I know! If I was able, I'd give you what you deserve!"

O'Casey merely wagged his tail, and decided that O'Banion still held evil thoughts. He would stay out of his way and hope that O'Banion would leave the ranch, and take the sad memories away. O'Casey knew, though, that his memories would not go away anytime soon. He had been hurt too badly for that relief.

O'Casey had extracted his crippling revenge, and he knew that the could have killed O'Banion, but that was not his plan! O'Casey wanted this mean and vile man to suffer for the rest of his time on earth. Suffer for Lady, and suffer for Little Ben. Suffer for the others, too! Those puppies were relatives! The guilty must suffer!

And O'Banion would suffer! He would carry his left arm in a sling for all of his years, and his left eye was never to see the light again. O'Banion's plight was only a bittersweet gratification for O'Casey, though. Little Ben was still gone. So was Lady. The other puppies, too. He had done what he felt was right to avenge an evil deed. Hate for O'Banion welled in every bone, and there was no pity either!

Still, there was one thing that did bother O'Casey, and it bothered him in no small way. The Irish Wolfhound, his breed, had always been known for their gentle natures, and never prone to attack without extreme provocation. The provocation to attack O'Banion was extreme, but was it necessary? It hadn't solved anything except to punish evil. O'Casey wanted to believe that punishing evil was enough reason for attacking so viciously, but in his heart was a feeling of shame. Not because of the suffering of O'Banion. That was just! The gentle and patient Irish Wolfhound breed was another matter, though. Had he sullied his ancestors great history as well as himself? This was a concern that O'Casey carried with him for all of his life, and he brought it when he came to Canine Heaven, too!

O'Casey lived a long, long time. He spent his summers at the ranch, winter months in the city. Pampered and loved devotedly by his Master, O'Casey could not complain. Neither could His Honor! O'Casey served, and he served well! He served long after Willy Boy was gone, too. He never forgot that first summer at the ranch. It would be an important memory forever, and even beyond! Particularly Little Ben!

Therefore, shortly after arriving in Canine Heaven, and learning there was a Puppy Community, O'Casey visited the area as soon as he could. This was also his first encounter with Lolita, an Afghan, who was as beautiful as she was arrogant and bossy. Lolita was the director of the Community, and wanted to know what O'Casey's intense inspection of a group of puppies meant. Visitors to the Compound usually showed no such scrutiny as that of O'Casey whose gaze followed the puppies fixedly. This was somewhat alarming to Lolita as she insisted on knowing O'Casey's concern.

"Please, Ma'am," he said. "I need to maybe look for someone ... you know maybe ... I reckon anyway ... a little fellow called Little Ben? Would you know?"

"Of course I would know one way or the other since I am The Puppy Community Director. We have quite a few Benjamins, however." Lolita replied in a casual voice.

"This wouldn't be Benjamin, Ma'am, I am sure. Just Little Ben." O'Casey was speaking slowly and sadly. "Would you please check. Just in case?"

"Well, I will certainly look in the files for you, Mr. O'Casey, when I can find the time. Right now we are in the middle of our morning play. Would you please excuse us? Make an appointment, Mr. O'Casey, and I will try to help."

This Irish Wolfhound was taking far too much of her time, and Lolita was a bit put out when O'Casey made no hasty retreat which she "fully expected".

"Well, Ma'am, I see that you do have a lot of help with the puppies, so can you check your files now? It would be a great kindness to me. You see I have waited so long to know."

O'Casey didn't want to appear to be unreasonable, but he was going to stand up to this arrogant, bossy and capable Afghan. So he was both surprised and a little heartened when Lolita paused in duties to address him once again.

"Very well, Sir, I will try to help you. If I don't, I don't know who else would have the authority since I am in charge here. Madeline, dear, would you please help with the puppies?" Lolita called to a frowning English Sheepdog.

"If you say so, Ma'am." Madeline was clearly not happy, and as she began to leave for the play area, Lolita opened the office door and beckoned to Madeline to join her inside.

"My dear," O'Casey could hear Lolita saying testily to Madeline, "Where are your manners? We have a visitor. I am shocked by your behavior! Where did your upbringing take place? Were you a farm animal of some sort?"

O'Casey didn't like what he was almost forced to hear, but he felt a bit better, even smiled, when Madeline retorted sharply:

"I was a DOG, Ma'am, same as all the rest of you! I am asking to be removed from the Puppy Compound, Ma'am, I don't like working here, and I never did!"

"You will surely get your wish, and very soon!" O'Casey heard Lolita say a little slowly as if she couldn't quite believe Madeline's attitude.

"My dear," Lolita continued, "It is most inappropriate to speak with such venom where the puppies might hear. I suggest that you return to your Community Director at once for guidance and reassignment. No one is welcome in the service of the puppies who will not be their champion to the exclusion of all other priorities and considerations."

"Oh, it ain't so much the puppies I don't like, Ma'am," said Madeline, "I'm good with them! I just don't like your treatment of Mr. O'Casey. He came like a kind and caring canine to ask you to help him 'cause he's hurtin' somethin' awful. I don't like workin' for you! I will leave now, but I'm hopin' you can help Mr. O'Casey, Ma'am."

When Madeline had gone, Lolita made the proper excuses for the delay while she called to Queenie, a cute Brittany Spaniel, to assist with the puppies.

"As you can see, Mr. O'Casey, there is little free time for requests such as yours without an appointment. Kindly remember our rules for any business other than observing the puppies playtime. Now, Mr. O'Casey, you have said, or I think you indicated, that this is a puppy known only as Little Ben. I am going to try to assist you although it is a very unusual request. Little Ben it is then?" Lolita asked irritably.

"Yes, Ma'am, and I thank you."

O'Casey continued to be polite. The visit to the Puppy Compound was maybe a big mistake! He didn't know at all anymore just what he expected, and sadly watched Lolita pawing through the files.

Lolita, meanwhile, had, to her surprise, found a Little Ben in the files in the L section: Crossbreed of Irish Wolfhound and Dalmatian. Scrutinizing O'Casey's huge Irish Wolfhound's make-up in ultra-gigantic proportions, made Lolita wonder if this might be the one that O'Casey sought. She also wondered if they might be related. If so, this had never happened before! Scary!

"Mr. O'Casey, would there be Dalmatian in this puppy's pedigree?" Lolita asked suspiciously.

"Oh, yes Ma'am! Yes Ma'am!"

O'Casey's heart leaped, and shaking all over, he bowed his head and waited for Lolita to say something. Just say something! Say anything! Please don't keep me waiting like this! But what if this is not the right puppy? Oh, Canis Major, please!

Lolita explained to O'Casey that if indeed this was the Little Ben that he was looking for, she must become aware of O'Casey's interest before releasing further information. After all, it was she, Lolita, who was in full and complete "charge" of the Puppies, and she did not take her responsibilities in a light and haphazard manner!

"Little Ben and I had the same father, Ma'am, an Irish Wolfhound. He is my younger half-brother. His mother is the Dalmatian in his pedigree."

"Then, I think we have found him. I do have to warn you, Mr. O'Casey, that Little Ben must not be aware of you, or of your interest in him. Too upsetting at this time, you know. He will be in line five, row three, in the second of the two groups just outside the fourth walkway. You may observe him there as long as you wish. That should be quite satisfying for you, Mr. O'Casey. Good-day, Sir. Just remember the rules."

"Oh, I don't want to do anything to upset your operation, Ma'am. This meant a lot to me. And I thank you again!"

"Good-day again, Mr. O'Casey!" Lolita said arrogantly turning to other matters. Looking up, though, she saw a bewildered O'Casey watching Little Ben through the open door, and showing not a sign of vacating the premises.

"Is there something else, Sir? This is a busy time for us. We have helped! Have we not? You will need to go on to the play area, and excuse us." Lolita said sharply.

Canine Heaven

"Please, Ma'am, I have found someone that I never expected to encounter unless he was here. He is my family, and I would like to know him ... have him to know me, you see. I don't quite understand the objection." O'Casey pleaded.

He wasn't going to let this capable and conceited canine ... this bossy and overbearing Afghan put him down like a nosy nincompoop! It wasn't fair! He had come in peace and good will seeking an answer to his troubled heart, and when he found Little Ben he was almost shut out! No, it wasn't fair. But on second thought, what could he do? Lolita was in charge of Little Ben the same as all the other puppies, and O'Casey decided that maybe he should not cross Lolita. Not now anyway! Take time to think.

So without waiting for Lolita's reply, O'Casey walked to where the puppy was going through his exercises. There were other visitors at the Compound as usual that morning. It was a very popular place in Canine Heaven. Everyone, or almost everyone anyway, enjoyed the puppies. Just remember the rules!

O'Casey hung around long enough to watch Little Ben go through the singing and dancing routine. Then it was a fun time frolic for the puppies who chased each other and rolled in the grass. As O'Casey watched Little Ben frisking about with such glee, it awakened memories of O'Banion's yard and the happy, happy summer playing with the puppy. A heart ache was awakened, too!

O'Casey thought of that sad morning when he had searched for Little Ben at O'Banion's cottage. He thought of Lady and her ordeal, and he thought about a different

63

roll in the grass ... the one with O'Banion. It was necessary but it still caused pain. But why should it?

O'Casey spoke to no one at the Compound while watching the puppies. His heart was too heavy for here was a joy in full view, and he was restricted by Lolita's unreasonable attitude, and no sense of family. Just as he had done on Earth so long ago, O'Casey gave thanks in his heart for what he still had, and went back to his duties at his office.

O'Casey did go again and again as a visitor to the Compound. He never made overtures to Little Ben or showed recognition of any kind. O'Casey's thoughts of "one day" ... maybe "one day"... maybe "one day" kept his spirits up to a degree, and he was both sad and happy at the same time. Lolita treated O'Casey with a cold detachment when he visited the Compound, but he no longer minded. There's always the power of the press, he told himself, but he didn't want to use it against Lolita just yet. Maybe later!

So, O'Casey cautioned himself to defer to this Afghan Lady as long as she controlled his relationship with Little Ben, That's if one could call Lolita's arrogance and restrictions a relationship! Still, it was all O'Casey had. A little something to be sure. He didn't want to lose it!

Consequently, O'Casey did not speak of Little Ben to the other residents of Canine Heaven. For to them, as always, O'Casey was the big Irish Wolfhound editor of the Canine Weekly who was outspoken, arrogant and not so easy to get along with or to know either. It never occurred to any of O'Casey's so-called associates that

O'Casey's heart, though sad, was a little happier now. It just had never occurred to any of them that O'Casey even had a heart! They did respect him though, for to upset O'Casey meant a scathing editorial aimed at an individual or maybe a whole breed. It was a well known fact that when on the attack, individuals and breeds were one and the same to O'Casey, and pawing on his typewriter, he held no venom back! He couldn't expect much support. Besides, no one knew anything about any of this. O'Casey couldn't talk. He was certain Lolita would say nothing.

But he wished somebody else could know and speak in his behalf. Madeline? No, probably not. For the first time since arriving in Canine Heaven, as important as he knew himself to be, O'Casey felt helpless. And very much alone.

The weeks went by with O'Casey busy at both the newspaper and on the lecture circuit. He went to the programed presentations given by the Puppy Community, and he visited there once each week. He always had lots to do, and it was no different this day. But he also had received a summons to The Big Bone Palace to meet with the Great Collie.

This was not so unusual for O'Casey had many meetings with His Greatness. After all, O'Casey was the editor of a very important publication, The Canine Weekly, so there was much business and consultation calling O'Casey to appear at the Palace. This was a special summons, though, and had nothing whatsoever to do with the newspaper! It puzzled O'Casey, but he was relieved. At least it wasn't a biting editorial upsetting to The Great Collie!

The meeting was a lengthy session, and when O'Casey departed the Palace, he was smiling. And later, back in his office at the newspaper, O'Casey began pawing on his keyboard writing an editorial to surpass all others. This was to be his masterpiece! It would appear in tomorrow's Canine Weekly along with The Yearly Report and the rest of the important news of Canine Heaven.

This morning, though, as the Bloodhounds, Buddy and Durkin, were busying themselves with The Yearly Report from the Palace, O'Casey was still writing, and rewriting his editorial. He would be late for Chapel as he often was but it just didn't matter today. This editorial was more important! So O'Casey wrote and rewrote, revised, changed or returned to his original text. Finally finishing and as proud of his work as a Pulitzer Prize winner, O'Casey locked his office, and prepared to leave for Chapel. O'Casey felt good!

Yes, O' Casey felt good. The pain and vitrol in the first writing of his editorial had been replaced with an olive branch. Very unlike O'Casey, who would never oblige or concede anything to a perceived opponent. This was a special case, he told himself, and he knew the arrogant Canine Weekly Editor would be back! So brushing his hair, and still smiling, O'Casey tossed a few jokes at Buddy and Durkin while making sure The Yearly Report was being processed. Of course the Bloodhounds were puzzled by this behavior but too busy to respond!

O'Casey was adjusting a fine dress-up collar on himself when he saw Carolyn and Lucy pass on their way to Chapel. They were late, too!

"There goes the pretty Carolyn." He called gaily through the open window.

"You ain't nothing but a big hound dog with two good eyes!" Carolyn smiled back at him and hurried down the walk.

O'Casey laughed and shook his head. That Carolyn was something else!

CAROLYN

Yes, Carolyn was indeed "something else"! She had always been "something else"! And she had earned the right to be "something else", or special, as she called her unique view of herself. Ask Carolyn! She will tell you that, yes, she is something special, and a pretty Black Labrador as well! She is not so likely, though, to speak of her family tree. Just nobody's business!

Carolyn couldn't remember how or why things happened as they did. She could remember an abandoned little Black Labrador puppy. In fact, she remembered a quartet of them. It was a memory which naturally began on Earth.

One cold morning, a shopkeeper busy with his daily deliveries, noticed four very young black puppies shivering and whining near his shop at the Mall. He looked around and seeing nothing, put the puppies in a box with wood shavings hoping this would keep them warm until someone claimed them. Leaving the box on the sidewalk, the shopkeeper went about his business.

The good hearted merchant could not know that the Mother of the puppies in the box was already more than a hundred miles away. She had been stolen in the night, and the thief had not noticed a small black fluffy mass lying with her in the kennel. When the thief tired of the puppies' crying, they were left at the deserted Mall. The thief's concern was the prize-winning female Labrador, Lady Queen, worth more than any of the other show dogs that he had seen being shown earlier in the year. He had not given any thought to the fact that Lady Queen might bear a litter of babies of grand, grand heritage! Biding his time to snatch the valuable animal had taken several months, and the thief couldn't know that a special pre-planned mating had occurred in that time period.

A liaison with Prince Rochambeau, a fine show dog of the same breed caused eight excellent specimens to arrive in the private kennel of Lady Queen. The puppies were equally divided with four going to each of the owners. The thief was surprised to find the four remaining puppies, but he was not smart! Had he been smarter, he would have decided that there must be a connection to the beautiful Lady Queen ... otherwise ... why would four puppies be sharing her private kennel? No rational thinking, and no compassion either! So abandoned one cold morning at a Shopping Mall by the greedy thief was a quartet of fine and valuable puppies!

The Mall began to come alive with a horde of shoppers and others that frequented its streets daily. The box was quiet with its occupants sleeping from exhaustion and hunger so little attention was given to it other than the usual smiles, ohs and ahs. As the morning wore on, some children gathered around the box watching the puppies and decided to place a sign on the box. It read "FREE PUPPIES". The children grew tired of waiting for someone to "take" a puppy, and scampered off.

There were no takers until Millie came along. She could use anything that was free. Even a puppy! Quickly scooping up the first one that she touched, Millie put it in her cart on a pile of rags and junk of every description, and pushed along on down the street.

Millie was a street person, well up in years. Senile and cranky as any old woman in her circumstances, Millie was kind and she loved the little homeless puppy right from the start. She was a frequent visitor around all the stores and cafes at the Mall. The waitresses in the cafes often gave Millie coffee, and paid for it themselves. This time, though, Millie needed more than a hot cup of coffee! Getting the eye of Amy, a favorite and generous waitress, Millie pointed to the sleeping black bundle in her cart now covered with something resembling a tattered lacy table cloth. Amy nodded through the window, and soon appeared on the sidewalk with a cup of warm milk.

Millie worked many restaurants over the next few weeks in the same manner. The employees were always kind. Black Carolyn thrived. Black Carolyn! A name so befitting for the puppy whose black coat shone even in the dark. Beautiful beyond words ... was the way Carolyn was described by everyone that saw the little princess-like canine riding in a cart filled with rags and junk!

All of this was a long time ago, and after an unsettling life, Carolyn came to Canine Heaven. Somewhere along the way, the Black had been dropped as part of her name. According to her, she was just Carolyn. Something special!

When Carolyn arrived in Canine Heaven, there was no welcoming committee to greet her at the Landing Site. No one, that is, except Hildegard who had been hastily recruited for the job since no Connections could be found for Carolyn in Canine Heaven. Pending her arrival, the usual search for Connections was a futile exercise. There were none! The new Whippet employee at the Palace was relieved of his job when Wrangler, The Chief of Staff, was made aware of this poor judgement. Sending Hildegard, the snooty and arrogant French Poodle, was a mistake to greet any incoming canine. To Carolyn, Hildegard was a disaster!

In the first place, Carolyn had no special regard for Poodles of any kind so she resented Hildegard from the beginning. Not that Hildegard was overly gracious. She wasn't! She simply could not imagine a canine coming to Canine Heaven without Connections, and Hildegard, after hearing Carolyn's uncultivated way of speaking, she was not the least civil. "A pretty canine, but low class." Hildegard thought. Carolyn was unimpressed. She knew her worth! But a pall fell over her heart just the same.

Carolyn had been told at the Briefing Center all the wonderful things awaiting her in Canine Heaven. Were all the canines like Hildegard? If so, why was she here among those who would only ridicule her speech and her commonness? She was not cultured, but smart, and she had served well, too! She was Carolyn! Something special! That, she knew was true! She didn't know how she knew. She just did! Then, why was this critter, Hildegard, being so mean, and so snooty? Couldn't

Hildegard see that Carolyn's fractured verbiage was not the whole canine? Couldn't Hildegard see?

Well, maybe Carolyn didn't belong in Canine Heaven. Maybe she had been sent here by mistake, but somehow she knew that she must stay. She sadly watched as the Big White Eagle spread his huge wings and flew away leaving her alone, and lonely with Hildegard! Hildegard, with her nose in the air, had said only a few words to Carolyn since greeting her with a cool, "Welcome Dear." A very sad Carolyn, however, walked with Hildegard to The Big Bone Palace where The Great Collie waited. His greeting was warm and kindly, and he was not aware of Carolyn's discomfort. All newcomers were a little shy at first!

Carolyn felt a bit better after the meeting with His Greatness, but only a very tiny bit! She didn't trust any of the other females, and stayed to herself. She had chosen not to be assigned to a position in Canine Heaven without first acquainting herself with "this" place where she was trapped. Just like on Earth! But here was a pretty place, and Earth had been a pretty place, too!

But Canine Heaven was supposed to be a reward! An honor that she had earned by serving well on Earth. Why then, did she feel so trapped? And alone? Carolyn didn't know! But she still had her dignity! She was Carolyn! They didn't like her here? Well, she didn't care! She would show 'em! Ever' one of 'em! Especially "them Poodles"!

So Carolyn kept to herself. Taking her meals and talking to no one. Going to Chapel and sitting alone. Spending time in the Library and Museum, or just walking in Fleecy Park. When her Community Director spoke about a position in Canine Heaven that she might like, Carolyn was not receptive. She wanted to know more about "this place", and a lot of other things, too, Carolyn told the Director without blinking an eye! The Director left her alone after that outburst, and the whole female population left Carolyn alone, too. After trying, as many of them did, to become acquainted, they grew weary of her attitude of aloofness, and backed off!

As the days went by, and Carolyn about as lonely as she could be, shared a few jokes with some of the males who teased her now and then. The male canines didn't seem to mind her fractured street way of speaking. Carolyn decided they were only interested in pretty females and speech and culture did not matter. Anyway, they were friendly, so might as well make the other females a little jealous! None of the Poodles, however, male or female, dared to talk to Carolyn about anything. The Poodles crossed the street when they saw Carolyn coming! They didn't need to! They were ignored anyway!

Even with the diversion of "jawing" with the males, Carolyn felt more and more the outcast of Canine Heaven. She did not take the time to reason, or to put anything in perspective. Intelligent she was, superbly so, and why she didn't quickly assess the very essence of Canine Heaven is beyond all reasoning in its self. Being so wrapped up in mistrust by her encounter with Hildegard at the Landing Site, Carolyn did not reason! She was Carolyn! Something special! She shouldn't have to reason! Not in Canine Heaven! Thinking was for survival and service on Earth, but not for some place called

Heaven! In fact, Carolyn didn't consider it at all! And she withdrew some more! So there!

If Carolyn had known that she could leave Canine Heaven, she would have in a hurry. A flight aboard the Big White Eagle "outta this place" would suit her just fine! Reasoning, of course, would have solved Carolyn's dilemma. Or most of it anyway. The Hildegard problem was already solved, but Carolyn was not aware that Wrangler had acted with such decisiveness in ousting the guilty employee. Hildegard's availability was a matter controlled, too! Carolyn didn't know about that either, but she would have been pleased. Someone had actually noticed her, and done something to help her! But she didn't know, and continued to grieve. Didn't anyone care? Anyone?

Yes, someone did care, and did something about it, too! Holy Joe had seen Carolyn in Chapel, and spoken with her several times. She always responded by being both shy and arrogant. Holy Joe knew about the situation involving the snooty French Poodle, Hildegard, and he knew that the Staffer at the Palace who caused it had been punished. But Carolyn should be laying this aside! Maybe she didn't know, though. Well, he would tell her, and he would tell Carolyn to make friends and enjoy all the wonders of Canine Heaven. What if her problems were of a deeper nature? Well, he would try to help her with them, too! All of this had gone on long enough!

So one warm morning, Holy Joe went looking for Carolyn. As he walked down the street, he was thinking of what he would say first. Here was a beautiful canine who truly walked in beauty, and with elegant grace as well! Right now, though, Carolyn truly walked with much sadness, too! How to break through? A real good question! How do you let her know that her queenly bearing, and intelligent demeanor was noticed by almost all of Canine Heaven's residents? How can you do that without seeming too patronizing? With her intelligence, it would be risky. With a chip on both of her shoulders already, Carolyn would see through that kind of talk right away! Then, what to do? Play it by ear? Yes! And proceed from there! See how it goes!

Holy Joe first went to the Library. Carolyn was not there. He checked the Museum. She was not there either so he crossed the sky bridge to Fleecy Park. And Holy Joe was still thinking of how to approach Carolyn once he found her!

The first thing, he decided, was to tell Carolyn something about the many kinds of canines here in Canine Heaven. Holy Joe was going to point out that a lot of them had fine pedigrees such as Hildegard claimed and bragged about. A great number, however, were of a mixed parentage, sometimes doubly so or even more! It did not matter, for all were equal in Canine Heaven. A purebred was no more important than a mongrel. They had all served!

Holy Joe also wanted to tell Carolyn that some of the canine population had been highly educated on Earth. Most of them, though, only minimally so. This did not matter either as each and every canine was placed or trained in a job or position of choice. Most preferred, however, to stay with their Earthly experiences in both learning and cultural endeavors. It all worked just fine!

But heck, why tell Carolyn this? It was evident that she must know by now! She had been in Canine Heaven for some time already. So, of course, she knew, and presumably quite well, what he was saying about the diversity in all matters pertaining to Canine Heaven. No, no need for that information. Just go with the play it by ear idea! Holy Joe prayed that it would work!

Carolyn was absentmindedly plunking the keys on the coral shell organ in the Recreation Center when Holy Joe caught up with her. She looked up, and smiled shyly as he approached.

"Hi, Padre." Carolyn said quietly.

"Well, good morning, Carolyn," Holy Joe smiled. "Care to go for a walk?"

"That'd be right nice," Carolyn was returning to her arrogant self as she spoke. "I like Fleecy Park a lot. Reminds me of the places where Millie and me went sometimes."

"Well, it is the fine Park in Canine Heaven, Carolyn. Built for all canines to enjoy. And we do!" Holy Joe said as they walked along the well-kept paths.

Carolyn giggled and chatted at her arrogant best. Arrogance was almost a habit now. But Holy Joe wasn't talking much. Just listening to Carolyn run on was enough, and he was thoughtfully in a satisfying mood. Getting Carolyn to open up was exactly what he was hoping for. So after a bit of banter and some well-chosen compliments, Holy Joe went straight to the heart of this meeting! Carolyn's relationship with the Canine Heaven population, and her aloofness.

"Carolyn, why do you find so little to make you happy here? You are not at all friendly with our females, and you are especially hard on the Poodles."

"No, I ain't!" Carolyn replied. "I just know they don't like me. They're jealous 'cause I know my way around up here. They think I don't belong! But I don't care what they think. Especially them Poodles who lived in fine houses. I ain't hard on 'em. I just see through their fluff, and know I'm smarter than them. Lots smarter! They wouldn't have made it on the streets like I did. Being pampered and babied and all dolled up with them ribbons. Yuk!"

"Well, I know some of them lived in pretty easy circumstances, but you belong here in Canine Heaven the same as they do." Holy Joe told Carolyn. "You served as well as they did, and we are all equal. And honored to be here! The Poodles or any other canine can't take away your right to be in Canine Heaven. But you know that already, Carolyn."

"Yeah, I know that! And I don't let it bother me too much 'cause I'm still smarter than any of them. Them Poodles especially!"

"You are smart, Carolyn, and pretty, too! We can all see that. But you must be lonely as well."

"No, I ain't!" Carolyn said sharply. "I ain't lonely! I go lots of places around here. I go to Chapel, and I go to the Museum and the Library, and I go to the Recreation Center a lot, too. And I joke some with the male canines. It's a little fun now and then. I ain't lonely at all, Padre!"

"Please call me Holy Joe, Carolyn. I am not a Padre. Only the Chaplain here. Holy Joe is my real name.

Anyway, about jawing with the male canines and ignoring the female residents, Carolyn, maybe isn't a good idea. Some of them will think you are loose being so pretty and all."

"Loose? I ain't loose! They're just being friendly! They don't nuzzle me! They know better! They're just fun to tease with sometimes. Ain't got nobody else to care 'bout me, Holy Joe. Whoever is saying that meanness ought to be 'shamed of theirself. They are just jealous 'cause I get the attention and they don't. I got more sense than any of them mean-talkin' canines. I ain't loose! Why'd you say that, Holy Joe?" Carolyn asked with a hurtful look, and her eyes began to water.

Holy Joe had not expected this outward show of feelings from the beautiful, arrogant and self-assured Carolyn who waited for him to speak. Holy Joe was silent for awhile as he considered this new twist in the mystery of Carolyn. Her dignity had been brought into question, and Holy Joe could see that now! Carolyn's dignity was real and it was natural. Nothing artificial. Something inherent and very tender. Maybe resulting from a fine pedigree. And it was certainly something that could not be altered by environment!

As Holy Joe walked quietly with the now silent Carolyn, he wished he could recall the words that had hurt her. In a way, though, an important door might have opened and better cleared what he was beginning to surmise. Carolyn is a special canine, he thought, very, very special. Just like she was always saying! Holy Joe started to speak but his words stuck in his throat when Carolyn quietly said:

"I ain't mad, Holy Joe. Just kinda numb knowin' you think them bad things 'bout me. You've always been real nice to me, and I was right proud when you asked me to go walkin'. But we must go back now. I reckon you've got 'portant things to do."

"I've got nothing to do today, Dear Friend, that is more important than my sincere interest in your acceptance of Canine Heaven, and of the honor to be here, Carolyn." Holy Joe told her." But I do want to tell you first that I am truly sorry for hurting your feelings. I did not intend to do so! Please forgive me! And please believe me, too!"

"It's alright, Holy Joe." Carolyn said in a resigned voice. "You maybe didn't mean it like that."

"No, Carolyn, I didn't! I'm trying to find answers, that's all. And I do thank you for your understanding! I'm hoping you will help me to know you a little better. Will you?"

"What do you want me do, Holy Joe? I don't know." Carolyn told him.

"Well, you can tell me some things, Carolyn, that I wonder about. For example, you mentioned the streets. Did you live on the streets?" asked Holy Joe.

"Yes, I did some of the time! Now you'll have a problem with that and I reckon you won't want to even know about me anymore. You don't want me to tell you! You don't want to know! Let it be, Holy Joe. Let's go back now." Carolyn begged.

"No, Carolyn, let's go forward! And I have no problem with your background on Earth. Why should I? There are canines here in Canine Heaven from every possible Earthly environment. And all of us have a story to tell. Sometimes we need to tell it to anyone that will listen. I believe this is true in your case, Carolyn, and I want to hear what it is in Canine Heaven that is perhaps not meeting your expectations. You are not happy here, and it goes beyond the ungracious treatment of you when Hildegard greeted you when you arrived in Canine Heaven. Hildegard was not qualified as a greeter, and the mistake is taken care of. The aide who was in error has been reassigned, and no longer works at the Palace. And all for you!" Holy Joe told Carolyn.

"For me? Gosh! I didn't know that!"

"Well, it's true! Perhaps, Carolyn, instead of continuing to be so sad and lonely, you might have sought out some answers on your own. I was there for a consultation at anytime you wished. It is what I do ... part of my job, but you did not seek my help. Carolyn, I want you to help me understand. Talk to me! And, Carolyn, maybe I will tell you about my life in the Hippy Commune when we walk another day."

"In a Hippy Commune?" Carolyn asked as if she didn't believe what Holy Joe had said. "You mean them guys who wore them rags on their heads?"

"Yes," Holy Joe smiled, "rags! Rags on their heads. Rags on their feet and backs, too! They were a great bunch of guys. Very good to me, and I was good to them. And good, in a way, for them as well!"

"Gosh!" exclaimed Carolyn. "I sure never would've thought that! You bein' so educated an' all."

"Well, they were educated, too, and loved intellectual challenges. I could not help but learn from them with such a varied exchange of ideas. It was an experience! A great experience! And I would not have changed it in any way!"

Holy Joe and Carolyn paused in their walk to rest on the warm grass that so abundantly and richly graced the Park. Holy Joe told Carolyn some of the wonders to be found in Fleecy Park that he thought she might have missed when she went walking alone. But Carolyn wasn't too interested! She already knew what Fleecy Park meant to her in her lonely afterlife, and it had become a special place indeed. Walking along its well kept paths and trails, Carolyn's heart felt a little lighter. And here on the soft grass, talking with Holy Joe, she was comfortable! He had actually lived with Hippies? And he had served them?

Carolyn had seen many Hippy men and women on the streets, and some of them did appear to be well-educated and had a touch of class although garbed in an unsanitary mess of rags. Others had no class, or grace either, so Millie said they were not real Hippies. Tom was a real Hippy, though! He was an artist!

Carolyn told Holy Joe about Tom who painted such "right nice pictures". He "spoke educated an' all, but kinda sad an' all, too". When Tom sold pictures, he bought Carolyn a nice T-bone steak, and a glass of wine for Millie. A real kind man, Carolyn said, and she decided that Tom was somewhat like the Hippies that Holy Joe knew. Yes?

"Yes," Holy Joe answered, "he probably was very much like them. My guys were not sad, though. You see, fifteen young men supporting each other made a difference. The whole idea, I thought, did have a sad theme.

For they pursued a dream that couldn't possibly be in a future for any of them. Buried inside each one was the burden of wealth, old family backgrounds of power and famous achievements. They could never lay all this aside."

"That is right sad, Holy Joe. Earth was funny in ways like that." Carolyn said. "So many had so much. More than they needed or could even use. So many had so little, and needed more to sort of break even. Didn't seem fair."

"No, Carolyn, it wasn't fair. Fairness is one of the beautiful truths in Canine Heaven, though! We do have that over Earth. And a lot more, too! And I know you will come to see that as well as the rest of us, Carolyn. And I have been talking too much! This walk is to benefit you, and not me! I don't come across many canines who have had exposure to the Hippy Culture, so I talked too much. Forgive me again, Carolyn. I guess that some-times I need to talk about my time on Earth, too. We all do! Gives us perspective, and we are a lot better prepared to both assess and accept the honor of Canine Heaven!"

"I enjoyed hearin' about your Hippy friends, Holy Joe." Carolyn told him. "Were they very dirty, too?"

"Filthy!" Holy Joe laughed. "I sure was cleaner than they were. I splashed around in the nearby lake a lot. They didn't!"

"You did? Splash in the lake? I did that, too! In the pond at the park for one whole summer. I was always lookin' so pretty, and my coat glistened sorta like a mir-ror. Millie would've been so proud."

"Tell me about Millie, Carolyn."

"Well," Carolyn said wistfully, "it maybe is not so special to know any of these things 'bout me. I know you want to help me, and I thank you, but maybe understandin' would be hard. And I am not educated enough to talk fancy like you do. Maybe Hildegard is right, maybe I don't belong here. Most everybody has got problems of some kind, though, and I ain't defeated if I got to be in this place. Here with so few friends I mean. Would be nice if I had made some friends, but I couldn't 'cause of what Hildegard said I reckon. I don't care, though, for I'll be alright, Holy Joe. I will be! I took charge of me when it was nobody but me, you know?

"You don't need to bother with me any more, and I thank you again, Holy Joe. Let's go on back now! I can't help bein' smart and I can't help bein' pretty, can I? I've had this feelin' that there is more about me that I should know, but I maybe ain't so special as I thought. But I am special! I ain't selfish neither! I am Carolyn! I ain't defeated!"

"No, Carolyn, you're not selfish or defeated either. And it is agreed that you are pretty and smart. And special, too! You spoke of a unique feeling you don't understand. Why don't you try to talk about it? Carolyn, I listen every day to problems of all kinds from canines of every breed. Like I told you, counseling and trying to smooth jagged edges is part of my job. Most of them come to me with their concerns, and we do what we can, but Carolyn, you chose not to seek my counsel. That's alright as far as your options go, but you are keeping too much inside. You will resolve all of this in time, Carolyn. In the meantime, I'm always there! We can go back to the village now if you want to." Holy Joe smiled, and then said as if in conclusion: "You know I did want to hear more about you, Carolyn! Your experiences on Earth appear to be from the left side of main street in events of what you'd call a natural life, you know. I was interested, not only for a helping talk, but to share more experiences of my Earthly existence. You see, Carolyn, these experiences were hardly mainstream. Unorthodox all the way!"

Carolyn was crying softly when Holy Joe finished talking. She did not know exactly why, and watching her saddened Holy Joe. He said nothing, though, and made no effort to vacate their seat on the grass in Fleecy Park either. Holy Joe had meant every word he had spoken to Carolyn. He liked her! He could see that she was indeed something special. Just like she said she was! How then, could matters pertaining to her gotten so out of balance in the few weeks she had been in Canine Heaven? Was Hildegard at fault? Well, partly! Hildegard had certainly stirred the cauldron! Aside from that, though, Carolyn didn't like any of "them Poodles", and wasn't that decided already on Earth? No, it went beyond Hildegard and her meanness to Carolyn. What then?

Holy Joe remained silent as Carolyn dabbed her eyes and blew her nose. She had expected more from Canine Heaven's promise of joy and love. Holy Joe knew this, but he didn't know just what her reasoning was. With the patience of an old Biblical character named Job, Holy Joe would keep trying. Carolyn may not want his help today, but maybe another time! On the other hand, though, maybe if Carolyn wasn't defeated, he was not going to be defeated either!

"Carolyn," he said gently, "we will leave now if you want. I still want to hear about Millie and you, though, but another day and another walk! Okay?"

"I want to tell you 'bout me if you really want me to, Holy Joe." Carolyn said, and then quickly added, "are you my friend now? I would like that!"

"Yes, Carolyn, I am your friend. It is an honor! I hope you are my friend, too. And yes, I want to hear what ever you want to tell me!" Holy Joe smiled as he answered Carolyn. Maybe this was it! Finally! Had he reached her or had she done the reaching? If so, that was alright, too! Let Carolyn be Carolyn, and let Carolyn take care of Carolyn!

"Please, Canis Major, just help her to understand her frustrations. Bring them to a manageable level of reality." Holy Joe prayed silently. "And if I am being used in some way, so be it! This girl must come to know Canine Heaven!"

But Carolyn appeared ready to talk, and this both heartened and amazed her companion. Holy Joe didn't urge, and a calmness fell over him. This was it!

"Well," Carolyn began in a wavering voice, "I ain't never had much of anything like them Poodles had, but I did have a lot of love. And I give my love to them that depended on me, too!"

"That's why you're here, Carolyn."

"Yeah, I reckon so! But comin' here I didn't know 'bout so I give a lot of love anyway to my Mistress. Millie was mighty good to me. As good as she was able to be with us livin' an' spendin' time on the streets an' all. Some said she was a "bag lady", but I never seen any bags. Just a push cart with a pile of junk in it. Millie did have a blanket, though, and we snuggled close together on them cold nights. I was all she had, and Millie would say this all the time over an' over. I never would have left her with her lovin' me so. I just couldn't! Millie called me Black Carolyn. I didn't like the Black part, you know, but I did like Carolyn. It's a right pretty name I think. Don't you think so, too, Holy Joe?"

"Carolyn is a beautiful name, and I think it fits you very well. And I also think that Millie was very lucky to have you, Carolyn." Holy Joe told her.

"Yes, I reckon, but I was lucky an' all to have her, too, with me bein' no more'n what I was."

"And what were you, Carolyn?" Holy Joe broke in. "What were you besides a beautiful Labrador canine?"

"Well, I don't rightly know. I just had these feelin's that I was special, you know, but maybe not. I wondered if I got displaced somehow. Like I said, though, Millie was good to me. So good that when she stole a can of soup, she would give me more than she took. When she was given some food, she'd give me most of that, too. She'd ask a butcher for a few bones for her "poor pooch"."

"That was kind of her."

"Yes, and the butcher give me right meaty bones, too! Eatin' so good keeps a canine's coat pretty and shiny. Mine was beautiful! And a kind doggy doctor who helped the street people gave me a shot or tonic when I needed it, and he fixed me, too. Well, you know 'bout it an' all, I reckon anyway. I never had fleas either. I was as smart lookin' a Black Labrador as you ever saw! I sure never had ribbons like them Poodles. A ribbon woulda been real nice you know, maybe at Christmas time. But I didn't ever get one."

"Well, I bet you were a pretty lady with or without ribbons."

"Yes, of course I was pretty! I was always pretty, you know! I do declare, Holy Joe!" Carolyn scolded. "I'm beginning to think that maybe you Do expect to talk more 'bout your own self. Here you are sayin', it will help me to come to terms, or somethin', to tell you about me, and I'm tryin' to 'commodate. I bet you never talked over your problems with anybody, Holy Joe!"

"Yikes!" Holy Joe said to himself, "I've done it again. I guess I've gone and touched her super ego or dignity a mite, or I've said something she don't like! Gotta keep her talking, and hope I can keep my foot out of my mouth!"

Holy Joe knew what Carolyn had said about him needing to talk more was exactly correct. He did like to talk and particularly about his days spent with his Hippy Masters. There was so little time for that, though. He was forever tending to the needs of others. It was his job, and he listened and counseled every day. Holy Joe loved smoothing a ragged edge for the canines who sought his help. And he loved Canine Heaven, too! He was perfectly contented!

Right now, Holy Joe guessed that he was making too many comments, and maybe it didn't suit Carolyn. He was only trying to show interest, and more than that, to keep leading her forward! She seemed eager enough now to share a lot of her experiences, and Holy Joe could see already that this was good. But he needed to know more. He still couldn't be sure of the feelings to which she kept alluding. How might these feelings hold Carolyn back? Were they important enough to keep her from fully appreciating Canine Heaven? And her honor to be here? Holy Joe didn't know! What to do now? Keep the comments to a minimum if possible. Ask more questions!

"What about Christmas, Carolyn? Did you ever get a Christmas present? You won't believe this, but I got five big rabbits for Christmas once!"

"Yes, I got a Christmas present one time." Carolyn said slowly, and perked up quickly when she realized what else Holy Joe had said. "Five rabbits? Why? Did you eat them? It ain't nice to eat little fluffy things, Holy Joe!"

"No, it isn't. And I didn't!" Holy Joe protested. "The rabbits were quite happy in their hutch. I could only observe them. It was fun!"

"Okay, Holy Joe, let me tell you about my Christmas present. It was real nice, too! They had a Christmas party, you know, for the street people. I was not allowed inside this big hall where the party was, but Millie went while I waited by the door. Well, a very mean person saw me standin' there, and said I must be a stray, so they better call the Pound before I bit somebody! Now I couldn't believe such meanness in some person, and at Christmas time, too! I just wanted to keep my eyes on Millie, an' to hear the pretty singin'. I went behind some trash cans 'til that dirty mean-talkin' person left an' went back inside. Just bein' mean at Christmas!

"Millie didn't eat with the rest. I watched for her, an' here she come out with a big plate of turkey an' ham an' beef with lots of other stuff, too. We went down the street to a covered warm place an' enjoyed our feast. It was so nice of Millie to tell me that she did not want to stay at the party with her best friend waitin' outside bein' cold and hungry an' all! Some kind old man come along an' throwed a silver dollar to Millie. She smiled at me with love; 'Black Carolyn, you got to have a nice Christmas present!' Well, she went inside the Dime Store an' bought me this little gold colored chain that I still wear. I wore it to Canine Heaven. See? Ain't it pretty, Holy Joe?"

"It's beautiful, Carolyn," Holy Joe smiled. "Millie loved you a lot to buy a gift for you instead of herself!"

"I reckon it's cheap, Holy Joe, The Dime Store stuff is, you know. But she was so happy when she put it 'round my neck. Millie said, 'Merry Christmas to Black Carolyn. She's all I got!' Well, I knew that! I've never had the chain off my neck since that Christmas Eve a long time ago. Millie used that other money from the dollar, you know, for a little sack of candy. We snuggled together under our blanket an' eat candy on Christmas. Just me an' Millie! That was how it was, Holy Joe. I had made a Happy Christmas for Millie 'cause, you know, I was just there! She had me to do something for. Give her a reason to celebrate. That's the right meanin' of Christmas. Somebody or something to do for! She couldn't do for me what them Poodles would have, though."

"Nevertheless, Carolyn, that's truly one of the most beautiful Christmas memories I have ever heard," Holy Joe said quietly, "and I've heard a lot of them, too!

You and Millie were wonderful! Especially you, Carolyn! So loyal and understanding and caring. I wonder if you ever knew yourself like that?"

"Well, of course, Holy Joe, I knew! I knew who I was! I didn't always want to do what I knew I had to do. I never wanted to do lots of things like bein' out on the streets so much. I did what I could to serve Millie 'cause she depended on me! I always knew who I was, and what I was, too! I wasn't stupid! What a thing to say, Holy Joe!"

Holy Joe didn't apologize, however. Carolyn's ego and sense of self were a given in this conversation! He let her outburst go unchallenged. He had had a feeling, though, right from the start, that something didn't fit. Maybe something important, and Holy Joe began to organize his suspicions. He might not be correct, but it was a start, and he wasn't ready to share his thoughts and give Carolyn something else to rail at him about. He was being patient and he was trying to help! Wasn't he? Yes! So he very gently asked another question.

"Carolyn, did you know your parents at all? I never knew mine."

"No, I never did know them. I just remember bein' in a box at the Mall. A sign on it said Free Puppies. I don't know nothin' else except I was in that box with three other puppies just like me. Nobody took any of us until Millie come along and put me in her cart. She never looked to see what I was. A girl or a boy. I reckon it didn't matter. I rode in the cart all warm an' fed real well, you know. I was treated good. It was 'cause Millie begged and stole for most of our food. I didn't like Millie doin' stealin', though!

"I would see them Poodles all fixed and dolled up with a fancy leash an' a pretty sweater. They would look at me in the cart among the rags an' sort of frown, you know. Their owners saw them lookin' at me, and pulled on the leash an' all sayin', 'Come, you might catch somethin' from that flea bag'. I never had no fleas! I was happy enough for I didn't know nothin' else. The sweaters them Poodles wore did have such pretty colors, though, Holy Joe."

"Would you have liked a sweater the same as theirs?" Holy Joe asked.

"No, I reckon not. I don't know! I never had one, but you know, Holy Joe, I had this feelin' that I was special, and every bit as good as them Poodles. I just had this feelin'! Now I wasn't ashamed of Millie, and I could ride in the cart an' feel like a princess, you know. I just had these feelin's that I deserved more. I had it pretty good! I wasn't complainin' about Millie in any way, though. But I had these feelin's, an' all."

Holy Joe could only surmise silently what he almost knew in his heart. A fine breed of Labrador must be in this sensitive canine's history. If somehow this was true, how did Carolyn come to be in a box at a Shopping Mall? It was a question to which Holy Joe wished he knew the answer, but more so, he hoped Carolyn might remember some event that proceeded the box at the Mall. He knew that Carolyn's personal record on file in The Big Bone Palace would show pedigree. Wrangler, Chief of Staff to The Great Collie, could help with this. He could not, however, be of any service, at least, in the matter of the box. If any information pertaining to this box became available, it would surely come from Carolyn herself! Holy Joe thought this was unlikely, but he still shared none of his suspicions with Carolyn at this point. Instead, he moved her forward, and urged her to continue.

"Millie did have a place to live. A little dingy house in a mess of others where mostly old folks lived. We spent more time on the streets than there at the house. Very often, Millie would be sayin' to me, 'Lets go out on the town for awhile, Black Carolyn'. She'd get out her cart and put on her old shabby coat and hat, and off we'd go!

"Millie would tell her neighbors about how she was goin' to visit with a son or daughter. She never had either one that I ever saw. When we'd get on back from bein' on the streets, Millie would tell her neighbors what a wonder it was to visit with her children. She never let them see her cart. I have no notion, Holy Joe, what there was 'bout the streets that kept Millie goin' all the time. Once we stayed out there all summer. And many winter months, too!

"Millie never had much money, but I remember we'd go back to her house and get her welfare check an' pay the rent an' all. Millie would lie again sayin' where we'd been visitin', an' off we'd go to be on the street awhile. And always to the meanest an' toughest place in the city, too! It just wasn't safe, but nobody bothered us much. They let old people alone. Mostly anyway. There was some, though, just mean and bad. I saw good things on the streets, but we saw much evil, too. An old woman ain't safe even with her dog. I guess me and Millie was lucky!

"Millie never talked much to anyone but me. She'd say over and over again, 'Black Carolyn, you all I got'. Sometimes she'd say, 'Albert don't care about me, and Pauline sure never did. I didn't know who she was talkin' about. Some folks, I guess, before my time.

"There come a time when Millie come down with a sickness, though. She sort of acted funny, couldn't remember, and at times didn't even know me! I kept a close watch on her doin' what I could, you know. But they hauled her off to a home of some kind. Nobody noticed that I was still there. The neighbors threw out a little food now and then. I kept waitin' for Millie to come home thinking she might remember me, and need my help again. New folks moved in the old house, and I knew there was nothin' at all there for me anymore. I didn't belong to nobody, you know. So I went on the streets again by myself, about sad and lonely as I could be!

"My coat was no longer brushed to a shine, and I hung around with a filthy bunch of dogs so I could eat. It just wasn't safe for me without Millie, and her image, you know. I was treated bad with nobody to sorta protect me, and I got to not likin' myself much for what I was becomin' just to eat and get along. I thought I might be losing some important thing like my dignity. And I needed my dignity! So I trotted off to a better part of town where the better city parks was, an' they was nice!

"It was summer, and folks come down to the parks for picnics. I got a lot of good food 'cause I was so friendly. And pretty, too, of course."

"Of course!" Holy Joe smiled.

"Well, I did splash and swim in the pond every night to keep myself clean. Then I would roll in the soft grass to polish my coat, you know, and my goodness, how it did shine! I was a pretty canine again. Millie would have been a little proud!"

"Yes, Carolyn, she would have! She knew you would make out alright, Carolyn. You took care of your-self as best you could. You were great!"

"Yeah, I was proud of me. But I was always proud of me, Holy Joe! I tried, and real hard, to keep me doin' right! Some fine folks was always comin' into the park, an' drivin' their Cadillacs, or maybe "Mercy-dees". Sometimes I ran an' jumped in, while hopin', you know, they'd take me with them to maybe some of their fine places like them Poodles lived in. And like I knew I de-served.

"They'd think I belonged to someone else, an' never took me. But it was acomin' to be winter time, an' I had to find somewhere to stay durin' the cold months. So I made friends with a park attendant, an' he took me home for his three kids to play with. I didn't know about the kids 'til I got there, and I felt sorta trapped, you know. I didn't like kids. I wasn't used to them. But, I did have to eat, Holy Joe, an' folks had stopped comin' for picnics so food was scarce. The park-worker was a kind man, but he thought I was a stray, and said so! This sorta hurt me, but I was a stray in a way I reckon. They saw my name plate on my little gold chain and it just said Carolyn. I never heard of Black Carolyn again, and I was glad of that, you know. I still missed Millie, though, an' remembered how she give me the little cheap chain with such love!

"The workin' family treated me kind enough, but I never liked them kids! I knew they sure liked me, though, wantin' to tousle me around an' wantin' me to fetch. Fetch! Can you believe it? Me fetch? I sure was no fetcher, and I was no roller-over or handshaker! All that common stuff wasn't me, and I was not common in other ways either! Them kids didn't know that, and hung on the back like monkeys. I never wanted any roots put down, you know, an' I wanted to stay 'til spring. They was good to me an' I was good to them! Even to the kids! But they were Blue Collar, and I needed more than that after them years on the streets with Millie. I wasn't a snob, Holy Joe. It was these feelin's I told you about. I just wanted to be what I was born to be, or at least who I thought I was supposed to be. Maybe I was selfish, Holy Joe, but I know it wasn't that!"

"No, you weren't selfish, Carolyn." Holy Joe told her." You aren't selfish now, and you will find the answers you seek. And I do believe that!"

"Well, I hope so! I am comfortable tellin' you about me, Holy Joe."

"And I am comfortable hearing it. I really am!" Holy Joe said tenderly.

"They was just a workin' family and with not much of anything. Just a poor man's table with meatloaf and lentils on week days, you know, an' a cake an' chicken on Sunday. Them kids would say to their Mama, 'Carolyn wants some ice cream an' another piece of cake'. And I would get it, too! Real kind folks.

"I kept feelin' that I was trapped, though, just like I got trapped when I was serving Millie. I loved her but I couldn't get away with honor, you see, and I would never leave anyone who depended on me like Millie did. I guess maybe I did have a selfish thought now and then. I kept thinkin' of them fine homes across the lake, and thinkin' if I could just get over the bridge, maybe I could find some good people lookin' for a fine Labrador like me. I was not able to do it by myself, though, I needed help, Holy Joe. The bridge was long and dangerous, you know!

"Anyway, I kept wishin' the workin' family would drive across the big lake in their pick-up truck, and I would be in the back of it by myself. Maybe I'm over there safe, jump out, an' look to findin' a fine new home, you know. But every time they went over the lake they would go in their old sedan car, and a kid would be hangin' on my neck. So it never happened!

"Then, I thought up somethin' else! Maybe nippin' one of them kids. Just a little, you know, to where they'd know I might not be safe around their kids, an' take me back to the park where the father had found me. And then I'd look for somethin' better. A real nice home like what them Poodles had! I was just as fine as them Poodles. Every bit! It hurt when they looked down on me! Even so, no matter my wantin' and deservin' more, too, Holy Joe, it just would not have been right to nip a kid to get away from the Blue Collar family. They had been good to me! They had took me in out of the cold! They had shared it all with me! Everything! They had even loved me as much as Millie did! I knew this, and I knew I couldn't leave them like that. So I settled down with them for quite a spell. But like I told you before, Holy Joe, I was trapped again! Just trapped! But I served long, and I served good, too!

"Then I come up here, and I reckon, or I guess anyway, maybe you don't see me as bein' anything special. Knowin' all these things about me, you may see only a street dog an' then a poor family's dog who wanted more, and who was just selfish! Guess that's been my big problem in gettin' along here. Do you reckon? We can go now, Holy Joe, and I do thank you." Carolyn said quietly.

"You're welcome, Carolyn, but we do have some unfinished business. And I, at least, want to attend to it." Holy Joe said. "I think we need to."

"Well," Carolyn replied, "I haven't anything else to tell you except I see that you was right, though, to want me to talk about things. It does help!"

Holy Joe saw Carolyn wipe a tear or two away, and he knew that telling her story had both helped and hurt her. It had been its own kind of therapy. Holy Joe understood now! His earlier suspicions were coming true. Carolyn was a special canine, and it was no surprise that she had come to Canine Heaven. It had been unsettling when her existence on Earth denied her being who she knew she was. Carolyn had always asked why.

Yes, she had always asked why! Only an ultra-sensitive canine would ever wonder so continuously. And only a special canine could have served two different households so faithfully while knowing they should be recognized as something other than just a loyal servant!

It was pretty clear to Holy Joe! An intelligent, caring canine as Carolyn, who had been given the honor of Canine Heaven, had expected more from it. She had expected recognition and verification of her pedigree. Of course Wrangler could help with this, but she did not know that. Carolyn hadn't tried to find ways to help herself! Since "this place was Heaven", she had expected to have her needs met. They hadn't been!

Carolyn didn't expect all that much now that Holy Joe thought about it. It was her hasty thinking that Hildegard, the snooty French Poodle, must represent Canine Heaven and its citizens. To be so wrong, bothered Holy Joe most of all as he pondered Carolyn's attitude. It didn't make a lot of sense. Hildegard should have been ignored! And she would have been cast aside had Carolyn been more certain of her own identity. This was her problem on Earth, and the quest for identity had followed her to Canine Heaven. So Carolyn's perception and sadness did make sense when viewed in that light! By sharing her Earthly memories, though, Holy Joe knew that a beautiful and arrogant Carolyn did understand herself better, as he himself understood her, and her problems, too!

Holy Joe was now ready to share his thoughts with Carolyn. The answer was Wrangler! They were going to see him, and get this identity question settled once and for all. Either way would be beneficial to Carolyn. She could lay a troubling notion aside, and devote her energies to accepting Canine Heaven as a great honor for loyal service. And, in Carolyn's case, the service was far over the "above and beyond" call. Holy Joe turned his attention to his crying companion. It had been a trying and emotional day for both of them!

"Carolyn, dear Carolyn," He said as though he felt her pain. "Did I not do right in urging you to talk about your memories? You said I was right. Please tell me why you cry if this is true. I have some ideas to talk about. I spoke of our unfinished business. Remember?"

"I remember." Carolyn answered. "It ain't that, Holy Joe. I don't know now what else you can say, but it makes me kinda sad thinkin' that maybe I didn't please you much with what I told about me, you know. I am still Carolyn! I am still special to me! I don't apologize either! I am proud of who I am, and as I told you, I will be alright. I ain't defeated! I reckon that's all I got to say except to thank you again. I guess I'll see you in Chapel. Let's go now!"

"We will not go anywhere right now, Carolyn, until you hear what I have to say!" Holy Joe said firmly. "You are a fine canine, and you know it! And you know also, that I am impressed by your strong character and sense of duty and your intelligence, too! I am proud also! Want to know why? Because I made a friend today. I think so anyway! I am sure hoping so! Now what more do I say to convince you of my sincerity and my desire to help you to be happy here? I know you have these feelings that maybe you were displaced on Earth. I feel you were, too. I think you need to put this concern to rest. We are going to see Wrangler at The Big Bone Palace. I am going with you now. Right now!"

"Goodness, Holy Joe!" Startled was the word to describe Carolyn's remark.

"Well, I meant every word I said to you." Holy Joe said calmly. "Now I believe you know who Wrangler is. If you read your copy of the Yearly Report, I know you do. Yes?"

"Of course not!" Carolyn replied in an irritated voice. "Why should I? No one explained anything to me, but I do know who Wrangler is. He is nice."

"Yes, he is, and he will help us to learn your pedigree, Carolyn."

"How?" Carolyn wanted to know.

"If you had read the Yearly Report, you would know that there is a file on every canine in Canine Heaven. And all files are sealed and only Wrangler, or The Great Collie himself has access to them. You have a file, too, Carolyn."

Holy Joe was explaining many things about Canine Heaven to Carolyn as they walked to The Big Bone Palace. It just didn't surprise Holy Joe that Carolyn, in her sadness, and snit, too, had not bothered to find out much about Canine Heaven. Like she said, why should she? She was Carolyn! Something special!

"And she is that!" Holy Joe said to himself. "Carolyn is special!"

As Carolyn and Holy Joe crossed the Sky Bridge, they met two Poodles going to Fleecy Park. They had pretty towels flung over their shoulders, and seemed to be headed for a swim in the pond. A popular place, the pond was! The Poodles smiled and waved to Holy Joe, and quickly swept by Carolyn.

"It figures," thought Holy Joe. He noted that Carolyn had ignored them as well!

Thinking about this, Holy Joe knew, and very well, too, that no matter how Carolyn had felt about the Poodles, the fact remained that she did want a ribbon, and she did want a pretty sweater like "them Poodles" wore on Earth. She hadn't had either! But that wasn't the Poodles fault! Holy Joe didn't mention the Poodles after waving back to them, and neither did Carolyn! They were in sight of The Big Bone Palace now. Holy Joe glanced at Carolyn as she kept her steps in rhythm with his, and trusting him all the way! Could he deliver? Oh please, Canis Major!

Once inside Wrangler's office, Holy Joe, after introducing Carolyn, wasted no time. He explained to Wrangler that the request to have Carolyn's file unsealed was a positive approach to this canine's sense of self and well-being. Wrangler agreed after hearing all that Holy Joe had to say. Carolyn remained silent as Wrangler with his usual proficiency, produced her file. Preparing to open it, Wrangler asked Carolyn the obvious question. Did she wish to have Holy Joe present to view its contents?

"Why, of course, Wrangler," Carolyn said. "Holy Joe suggested this. That's sure a strange question."

"No, Carolyn, it isn't strange. You have rights here, and complete privacy where this document is concerned! May we proceed then?"

"Please, Wrangler, don't let's wait any longer. I didn't know about any of this before, and now maybe I can learn who I am," Carolyn tearfully pleaded.

"Very well," smiled Wrangler. "I am beginning now: ... It is officially recorded that Carolyn is a purebred Labrador Retriever. Black! This canine is certain of a fine pedigree! ... Parents no-doubt were prized show canines. It is decided thusly for Carolyn is near perfect in every way. Good legs. A fine head with ears, eyes and muzzle in almost perfect balance. Splendidly so!

"Carolyn's coat is thick and shiny. Her feet are well-padded with the toes properly set. Beautiful tooth system, and tail at the proper angle. A very, very remarkable intelligence! Our own testing of this canine proves the proceeding information to be correct. In summary, Carolyn is an excellent testimonial to the great history of a fine canine class, the Black Labrador!"

"It says that?" Carolyn asked.

"Yes, that's what it says, Carolyn, and it seems you have a fine pedigree, and an outstanding history as well."

Wrangler told Carolyn this in a reassuring voice, but he knew that there was no surprise for her with what they had found in her record. Nevertheless, Wrangler felt good! He had helped in a special way. No matter Carolyn's private reaction, she still needed to see the information in her file.

Wrangler saw what Holy Joe had been observing all day while talking with a reluctant Carolyn. Wrangler, like Holy Joe, saw beyond Carolyn's physical elegance and arrogant manner, and looked into a beautiful character! Yes, this canine was special. Holy Joe was right to ask for his help.

Carolyn was silent as she looked at the file which Wrangler had placed in her paws. Her feelings had been right, and even though she knew this already, the knowledge was sobering to actually hear it put into words. And this file! It was real! What was she to do? What was she expected to do? Think? Yes!

Carolyn reached as far back in her memory as she could. It would not take her past the box with the shavings and the bread and the three companions who looked just like her. It was no use!

Carolyn's memory always moved forward to Millie, the streets, the park, the working family, and the duty connected with each one. The duty and the loyalty! Both were always there laying like a rock on her heart. There was no escape. Carolyn was what she was. She couldn't help that! And being who she was, she reasoned, had gotten her past difficult times. In other words it had "seen" her through! Not the way Carolyn would have chosen. No! A thousand times no! But through just the same.

Seeing Carolyn lost in a quiet reverie, both Holy Joe and Wrangler knew, or thought they did, what she must be thinking. Well, they did not know! And no one would ever know either! Carolyn couldn't say what it was all about her self. It was true she had shared many soul-wrenching thoughts with Holy Joe, but this duty and loyalty thing wasn't something that she could communicate. She did not know how! Now couldn't her new friends, Holy Joe and Wrangler, see that learning the secrets in her file, had not affected Carolyn in the usual way. Why get excited about things that one already knew? Carolyn was Carolyn!

Carolyn smiled. Thinking it was expected of her after all the help given to her this day. Holy Joe and Wrangler smiled, too. Their spirits were high!

Holy Joe thanked Wrangler and shook paws with his good friend. A fine job!

"Well, Carolyn?" Holy Joe asked as they walked toward the Village.

"Gee, Holy Joe, it's right nice. At least I reckon it is about me having a fine Mama and Papa. I sorta knew that already. I really did, Holy Joe."

"I know you did, Carolyn. I know it very well now! But you also needed for others to know it, too. You needed to have your pedigree officially known. I didn't need to know. Canine Heaven did not need to know either! Your serving, not your pedigree, brought you here to this fine reward. Your feelings of who you thought you might be can be laid a long way back in your memory. Now you know! It's a new day, Carolyn. Aren't you glad that you know? Officially?"

"Yeah, I reckon so," Carolyn slowly replied. "But I do wonder how come our Mama to leave us at some Shopping Mall with her bein' so fine an' all."

"She wouldn't have, Carolyn, if she had a choice. You will never know why, and you don't need to know. You really survived very well! You aren't bitter, are you?" Holy Joe asked.

"Oh, gosh no, Holy Joe! I wouldn't be bitter an' frettin' about things of which I couldn't control. Bitter? No I ain't bitter! Goodness, Holy Joe, what you can think up! You amaze me! I did gain so much in the life I had. I know I did learn on the streets. And I had learnin' with the poor workin' family, too. Maybe I didn't learn a lot of educational or cultural things, but I am not bitter! Learnin' is learnin', Holy Joe, an' all learnin' has value.

Look, I know a few fine words, you know! And I had more class than most canines do. I had class! I had a lot of class!"

"And you still do!" Holy Joe smiled warmly at Carolyn. "And you are simply wonderful, and a wonder as well!"

"Thank you for that, Holy Joe. That was nice of you, and thank you for all the time you spent with me today. I am thinking you did prove helpful. Bein' educated an' all is good I reckon, and I aim to do more readin' and learn how to use the Library things better. I do enjoy the Library! Holy Joe, I am not aimin' to brag about my parents an' my fine pedigree. It's private business! Don't you think so?"

"Yes, it is, Carolyn! You said that you enjoyed the Library. Maybe you can be assigned to a position there. Since you are not yet assigned, I could perhaps suggest it. Would you like to be assigned to the Library?" Holy Joe inquired.

Carolyn's face lit up! "I'd like it a lot, an' I'm smart an' I'm quick. My speech ain't so good, though, and maybe that would make a difference until, you know, I could improve it, and I do mean to learn lots of things. But I am Carolyn! Now my fine pedigree is fine, an' all that, but I won't forget where I come from an' what my life was like! That experience made me what I am, and my speech and grammar is a part of it, an' I won't turn my back on it! I want to learn an' be educated. I always did want that, Holy Joe. Always! I was not able to do this the way it turned out, but I learned as much as I could. I am proud of me, and proud of who I am. So bein' all this, I won't be what others might like to see. I am Carolyn!

Somethin' special! I do want to be in that Library, Holy Joe. But I won't pretend to be nothin' else. Just me! Now, will my speech make a difference?"

Holy Joe heard the wistfulness, and he heard Carolyn's determination, too! She would not sacrifice her loyalty to those she had served on Earth. And she would go unbowed as well! Since he had advanced the idea of a position in the Library for Carolyn, Holy Joe knew she would find a way to obtain it, and not give up anything that was important to her. Or offensive either! And she said that HE amazed her! But he had spoken. Now he must deliver the position somehow. And Carolyn, it seemed, had taken his suggestion to be a "done deal".

For once, Holy Joe was glad that he did have a little clout in Canine Heaven. Along with the irascible O'Casey, and the ever dependable Wrangler, Holy Joe was known as one of The Big Three. This exalted trio answered only to The Great Collie. They were his ear to the general population of Canine Heaven. A more efficient group could not be had, and His Greatness trusted them without question. They worked well together so Holy Joe saw no big problems. Wrangler would agree to Carolyn being placed in the Library. O'Casey probably would go along, too!

Now to answer Carolyn's question of her speech. Would her manner of speaking make her a liability should she be assigned to the Library?

"Not at all!" Holy Joe assured her. "Not at all, Carolyn, for you will encounter the idioms and dialects of all breeds of canines. You will not be in a minority situation. You do like?"

"I really do, Holy Joe! I reckon I really do!" Carolyn said smiling. "I'm going to be the very best!"

Holy Joe didn't doubt that! He also noted that Carolyn had smiled, and for the first time that long and emotional day. Holy Joe felt good!

"Holy Joe?" Carolyn called as they parted, "Remember now, I want to hear some more about them Hippies!"

Holy Joe laughed and waved good-bye to Carolyn. He entered the Mess Hall.

He was exhausted, though. He could not remember another canine giving him as much trouble in trying to help them as Carolyn had. Yes, the day had been productive. But for who? Carolyn would have solved her problems in time without his help! So in the end, Holy Joe knew that he had learned and benefited every bit as much as Carolyn did. Yet he still felt good about it all! Quite special, Carolyn was. Quite!

Holy Joe kept his word and did suggest that Carolyn be assigned to a position in the Library. This was done, and much to Carolyn's joy. She thought she belonged where her smartness would be useful. That place was the Library! Carolyn blossomed, and made friends by being helpful to all of the canines. A request for a book or any Library service was a pleasure for Carolyn. Other females still did not understand Carolyn's high opinion of herself, but she was accepted as one of them.

Holy Joe, as was usual anyway, made frequent visits to the Library. He saw Carolyn performing her duties with efficiency and pleasure. She was always glad to see him. They had become great friends. And this was almost all that Holy Joe could be certain of their day spent in Fleecy Park. Carolyn was very much his friend! He still thought the telling of her story had been helpful, and he still thought that it was good, too, for Carolyn to know for sure just what her pedigree really was. Holy Joe didn't know how Carolyn really felt about this information. She hadn't even mentioned it again! Holy Joe reasoned, though, that Carolyn was Carolyn! And still an enigma in Canine Heaven!

Holy Joe would smile sometimes when he saw Carolyn attending to a Poodle's request for service. She was so polite and helpful that the Poodles were saying how nice the new Library Lady was! While Carolyn couldn't fully embrace a Poodle of any kind, she would never be unfaithful to her Library duties. Holy Joe was amused by it all! A beautiful, beautiful irony!

Carolyn had moved up. Her smartness and determination had paid off. In no time at all, her position had been upgraded to First Assistant to Lucy, the Head Librarian. Carolyn had learned a lot since coming to the Library, and a great amount of time was spent reading almost anything. Lucy's super learning level, and her patience, too, did much to benefit Carolyn in her quest. These two, Lucy and Carolyn, were becoming a good working team. They admired one another, and got along great! They were friends outside of the Library, too.

With her new found knowledge, Carolyn's enunciation improved. She hadn't planned it that way, though. Learning was her goal. Not perfect diction! And as she had told Holy Joe that long day in Fleecy Park, she would not change a bit from what she was. But in the natural

Lodean Mallamo

order which was inevitable, Carolyn's speech had changed. She gave no great notice to this, and it was still "them Poodles". Some things just would not go away! They didn't have to! This canine had already done alright by her self, and she intended to do more with each opportunity that came her way. It was because she "reckoned" she liked a place called Canine Heaven, and Canine Heaven, she "reckoned" also, was lucky to have her. She was Carolyn!

This morning in Chapel, as Holy Joe surveyed his "flock" of worshipers, he noticed Carolyn and Lucy quietly enter the Chapel. They were late! Both were smiling as they made room in their pew for O'Casey. He had hurried in late as well. All three knew that Holy Joe had seen their tardiness, and did not look at him directly. They squirmed busily!

Holy Joe was observing Carolyn more than the other two, though. She seemed so happy! She had been interviewed for the position of Most Private Secretary to The Great Collie. Beautiful!

HOLY JOE

Holy Joe saw Jetaway walking around outside the Chapel this morning. Jetaway looked very worried, and very sad, too! Holy Joe wanted to see if he maybe could be of help, but the choir was already singing its first hymn, and he himself would be speaking shortly. No, Holy Joe could not leave the Chapel at this time. He made a mental note, however, to seek out Jetaway just as soon as the services were over. It was the best he could do!

Holy Joe knew that Jetaway had lost his wings again; a frequent occurrence with this canine. Holy Joe also knew a summons had been issued for Jetaway to meet with The Great Collie today. The wing-loss would not be a matter of importance to His Greatness. A wing-loss was trivial in Canine Heaven. It happened all the time! So the summons was for something else, and that something was obviously very hurtful to Jetaway.

And on this particular morning, the good Chaplain of Canine Heaven went about his Chapel duties with Jetaway on his mind, And in his heart, too! Canis Major? Please!

Holy Joe was like that! Whether it was tending to the spiritual needs, or just being available, Holy Joe was always there for his "flock". He was the most popular and best loved of all the Chaplains that Canine Heaven had known through the years. And there had been many fine and pious canines who served in that exalted position. All of them admired and respected. There was just something about Holy Joe, though! And not a single canine could say why they all liked him so much. They just did!

Holy Joe was strong, dependable and intelligent. He was probably the best educated canine in Canine Heaven. This was because of his experience on Earth living in a Hippy Commune with fifteen smart, well-educated and wealthy young men. They had nothing to do except to indulge their Hippy status. And learn! Holy Joe learned along with them. They studied everything! Holy Joe learned a lot about everything, too! Questioning everything as well! He had discovered exploratory knowledge all by himself!

The Hippies would have been so full of themselves had they known that Holy Joe, under their influence, had become one smart little "Hippy". And he had!

Even in Canine Heaven, Holy Joe did not accept anything at face value. Instead, he analyzed, deducted, supposed and tested. Wrangler teased Holy Joe a lot about this approach, and he teased Holy Joe about The Great Charter, too. They both had an interest in that mysterious document! Together, they would find its secret, they said. That's if there really was a secret! Until they knew, though, Holy Joe would be asking questions, and Wrangler would continue to tease even as he had many questions of his own. These two intelligent guys were good friends.

Wrangler, of course, worked for The Great Collie as his Chief of Staff. He had access to The Great Charter at all times, and shared what information was available with Holy Joe. Nothing would satisfy Holy Joe greatly for he always wanted to know more. Wrangler was very interested, too, but not like Holy Joe whose questions had few answers! Holy Joe had an insatiable desire to learn, and about anything and everything! It was little wonder that Wrangler teased Holy Joe, The Scholar, so much! That's what Wrangler called his friend when a debate could not be settled. This was all in good fun, and Holy Joe took the teasing in stride. In fact, he had two or three questions to ask Wrangler!

Holy Joe didn't really know much about Wrangler's life on Earth. He had never spoken of it to Holy Joe, or any other canine as far as Holy Joe and another good friend of Wrangler's could tell. Come to think of it, neither had Holy Joe shared his most important remembrances with his fellow canines. Of course his being raised in a Hippy oriented environment was well-known. And O'Casey had even written the ugly editorial condemning Holy Joe's lack of a proper background to be Chaplain of an exalted place such as Canine Heaven! A bit nasty, but the canines had grown a little tired of O'Casey's abuse of his "Freedom of the Press" cry to excuse a bias. So nobody paid any attention. It was just meanness! Holy Joe didn't respond to the editorial either. He had no secrets! Wrangler probably had none either.

Being such close friends, it seemed to Holy Joe that he and Wrangler would talk more about themselves. Their conversations were either academic or The Great

Charter mystery. Holy Joe talked more than Wrangler did anyway, and was more apt to mention an event that happened on Earth. Wrangler would stay on the topic being discussed, and not respond with a tidbit of his own. Like Holy Joe, Wrangler was busy almost all of the time. He was seldom seen without his clipboard, and ready to serve The Great Collie or take care of other Palace business. Oh well, one of these days they'd get around to having a yap about themselves! Maybe when they had deciphered The Great Charter of Canine Heaven! Right now, though, they had a shared interest in this document and a visit down memory lane would just have to wait!

Wrangler had told Holy Joe all that he himself had learned about The Great Charter. There were those questions of doubt from Holy Joe, though! Wrangler tried to answer the best he could. He explained that erasing a canine's memory for four months prior to his leaving Earth was because knowledge of his departure was unnecessary. The canine served and earned the reward of Canine Heaven. How or why he got here was not important. Holy Joe understood all of that! He agreed with it! His chief interest was the coded parts of the document, and Wrangler couldn't help with that. Not yet anyway!

No, Holy Joe had no problems at all with his four month memory erasure. He was smart enough to see the benefit in the stipulation for all the residents. They still had plenty of memories! And they treasured them. Holy Joe, too!

Those guys in the Commune were just great! And Holy Joe knew he had served them well, but they had served him also. Often chuckling to himself, he remembered the fellowship, the wonderful learning experiences, the love flowing so freely, the freedom to grow and the fun, too! And it was all good! He sure hoped his Hippy Masters continued with their learning and got back in school.

Holy Joe was very content in Canine Heaven. He had no special need to know anything about his arrival there. And, of course, he wouldn't!

Strangely enough, it was the demise of Holy Joe from Earth that caused one of the most unbelievable events in the history of any canine. The information was not recorded in Holy Joe's private file in The Big Bone Palace, and never would be! He did not need to know according to The Great Charter. But had he known of the event, he would likely have been amused for nothing ever happened in the Commune that was any surprise to him. Those guys! But once again, Holy Joe would have seen love! A great, great love, and all for him! He didn't need to know!

And he didn't! But he remembered!

One of Holy Joe's earliest memories was riding in a basket on the front of a big and noisy motorcycle. The breeze ruffled his hair and tickled his nose, but the cycle only slowed when it came to the dusty lane that led to the Commune. Those rides were fun times. The guys residing in the Commune were fun, too. They were real Hippies they said, and proud of it! They had a goal!

Holy Joe's friends and Masters were college students, or they had been before taking time off to find the meaning of life and their place in the big universe. The universe was especially important to them. They had many discussions about it as well as all sorts of intriguing phenomena that might explain their existence. They had a lot of questions! And real Hippies asked a lot of questions, too!

This was the nineteen-sixties. The decade of questioning. The decade of a restless rebellion among the young who waded through a psychological maze not understanding where they were in their quest. It was a decade of dropping in. A decade of dropping out. And a decade where the established citizenry didn't know what to do about any of it! Holy Joe did though. He enjoyed it all!

The Commune residents acquired Holy Joe as payment in full by the owner of a pet store who had supposedly damaged their old wooden cart. The cart, used to haul food and supplies from town to the Commune, was left at the curb near the pet store as the Hippies did their shopping elsewhere. The well fed mule, hitched to the cart, waited patiently.

The cart was outdated, but usable and very necessary. Absolutely no cars were allowed in the Commune. Not good for the environment, the young Hippies said. They didn't worry much about the old motorcycle, though, with its spewing pollutants. No problem there!

The owner of the pet shop had moved the cart and mule from the entrance to his store after becoming rather miffed by the waters of the bloated mule that flooded the sidewalk and splattered against his doorway. He only moved it a short distance, and no damage could be readily seen. Several of the previous law students at the Commune didn't appreciate the misappropriation of their property as they called the store owners action. They had work to do!

Citing codes pertaining to property rights and law, the case was presented to the shopkeeper in strong legal language. This was scary enough! But the monetary figures demanded were really, really frightening! After he nervously explained that he could not pay the amount asked for a cart already in disrepair, the store owner offered them a puppy. It was a purebred Irish Setter, he told them, and he couldn't do more!

The Hippies accepted the puppy, and promised to let the matter drop. Most of the town's citizens didn't like the Commune being so near, but they were a bit in awe of it, too! They were somewhat fearful as well, and they did not know exactly why. The Hippies bothered no-one, and their presence at the Commune was legal. The young law students had taken care of that! Nothing could be done, but the town's uneasiness was a fact. It was no wonder then that the pet shop owner was happy to settle the cart incident with the Commune members for only the price of a puppy!

The Hippies were happy, too! A real little Hippy, the puppy was! They gave him the name of Holy Joe, and how they did love him, and spoil him, and cater to him in every way possible! Holy Joe was a beautiful plaything, and reminded the young men of playing with their pets in earlier days. They had been so busy with the activity in the Commune, and their new-found freedom, too, that they had forgotten what a delight that a little puppy could be. Holy Joe grew and thrived in this environment!

Real Hippies, as they proudly said, came only from wealthy backgrounds and could afford the luxury of debate with contemplation. In fact, their wealthy families were happy enough to provide, and to support the Commune in every way they could. They knew this idea was an unreal effort to calm the restlessness of the times, and if sanctioned, would soon run its course. The parents hoped their offspring would hurry and "find" themselves and get back in school. The young men must be prepared to take the reins, at some point, and guide family firms and corporations. And it was expected! Therefore, no shortage of cash flowing to the Commune. But the young men had no plans to leave the Commune, and seldom contacted their families at all. They were Hippies now! They had a goal!

In order to pursue the goal, it was necessary to forgo certain established behavior along with other rituals such as toiletry. So they didn't bathe, and they didn't shave. They let their hair grow long, and tied a bandana on their head. Holy Joe had his own little bandana knotted around his neck. He was a Hippy, too! And proud of it!

How could one find his place in the universe, the young men reasoned, in a business suit and tie? Well, he simply couldn't! So they wore their torn and dirty shirts, cut-off jeans and ragged sandals. And how could anyone with any educated leaning work through problems with a hopped-up brain? Holy Joe's new friends looked down on the drug users. They were not Hippies! Merely confused bums with no learning agenda! None of them were welcome at the Commune. Holy Joe loved the Hippies for that stance, and he loved them for themselves, too! He was always wondering what interesting project they would tackle next.

Well, they decided to put in a garden and grow their vegetables. So much better for them than pesticide treated produce from town, they said. And lots better for the environment, too! Their gardening skills, however, were not so good, and this effort was not successful. So it was back to Pesticide City!

In an attempt to beautify the area, the Hippies planted a rose bush. Quite a bit more productive than the garden, the bush grew and blossomed profusely. Its beautiful white flowers filled the air with a delightful fragrance. Holy Joe lifted his leg to the bush several times each day, and it was still white with roses! This surprised the Commune residents, as two of them had had some classes in botany. Not enough, though, to benefit the vegetable growing! They said Holy Joe must like the sweet odor of the roses, so it was alright to use the bush for any purpose he chose. In fact, anything that Holy Joe chose was just fine, and he "chose" everything!

The young men's sleeping bags had a distinct "ripeness", but Holy Joe used them all! A different one each night. He slept with all of them. And he was always welcome. Just whatever Holy Joe wanted! And he sat at the old rickety table with them for meals. Since money was no concern, the food was the best. Steak, lobster, or whatever, it was available. Caviar and wine with imported crackers and imported cheese made a fine menu! Holy Joe dined with gusto! He also enjoyed a taste of brandy from their cups, and he helped himself from their plates as well. He was welcome! He had an unusual, but happy life.

The young men were happy, too. They shared the same goals. There were fifteen of them, and they got along well. This is nice, they said to each other. We will find our place in the universe and the meaning of life right here! So they debated, and they contemplated on their ideas and positions. All universal, of course!

Holy Joe watched the young men. He listened and he learned. He thought he must be the smartest pooch in the universe. Holy Joe had observed the local canines obediently following orders as they were told to heel and sit. It all was so utterly boring! Those poor animals should be thinking for themselves in a disciplined fashion, he reasoned, and they should know about Plato, Aristotle and Socrates. And Hobbes, too, and all the other great thinkers! And, they probably never even heard of Galileo, or Copernicus either. How sad!

Holy Joe knew his life-style wasn't conventional, but he had everything! A huge part of that "everything" was the discipline and knowledge he learned at the Commune. Who needed a weekly bath, or a daily walk? He could swim in the nearby lake, and run free. He was not a house pet! He was a Hippy! He loved learning, and there was much more that he should know. He was ready for a new challenge, and he wondered what it was going to be!

What discipline would come next to be passionately embraced? What problem hadn't these guys tackled yet? Their quest, of course, was on-going ... a matter to be resolved; wherever they had to go! Well, Holy Joe's intensely motivated friends were going to debate deity based religions. Holy Joe wanted to learn about everything! Religion?

Yes, religion! The young men, after much soul-searching, meditation and an introspective debate, decided that the most likely answer to their quest must be deity related. They had already explored almost everything else! A study of the world's great religions was undertaken at once.

They ordered books, papers and lots of Bibles. They gave themselves Biblical names. They remarked how wonderful that Holy Joe already had his Biblical title. The name that they gave to him, they said, was a miracle! A great power was leading them! And they had not recognized it! A miracle! They understood now! Holy Joe was there to lead, and to show them the way! Thus, he became a symbol of light, love, and joy! Holy Joe was all these things already, but now they had taken on a different, and very special meaning!

The scripture and its messages were about the only topics discussed at the Commune now. Gideon, Moses, Jacob, Gabriel, Joshua, Hosea, and other chosen Biblical names were used almost exclusively. Gideon was a talented speaker, and Moses was a great leader. The others followed and learned. But Holy Joe thought the young men were going a bit overboard in this religion matter. He wanted to learn about it, too, but not with such undisciplined intensity as it seemed they were doing! It was scary! And Holy Joe wondered if the fun times at the Commune were over.

The playful fun times were not over at all! Holy Joe still got all the attention he needed. And then some!

The Hippies loved Holy Joe as much as they did each other. He was a Hippy, too! A precious little brother. Holy Joe had more than any canine could need. There were balls and frisbees, and plenty of toys and stuffed animals to tear apart at will. Holy Joe had a wagon and harness set. Some stray cats were brought to the Commune so he could chase them. The cats took refuge in the trees, and left the area when everyone was bedded down. Particularly Holy Joe!

Holy Joe was presented with a hutch of five white rabbits for Christmas. A special seat on the motorcycle was also provided for him. His needs were so important at the Commune! While their religious convictions were of worth in the young men's quest, Holy Joe was of greater value. He was their symbol for all things good! So they gave him all the good food and let him lap the wine and brandy and coffee from their cups. It was a strange existence in the Commune for both man and canine. And one day it ended!

A careening car. A boy of fourteen. A stolen vehicle. A Commune already at rest. And Holy Joe was no more!

The grief and anger ensuing, caused the boy's father, a doctor, and also a political czar in the town, to prepare the necessary forms acknowledging that an accident had occurred, and a fatality had resulted. The doctor made not even one inspection! In his hasty desire to protect his son as well as his own political standing in the community, the doctor spoke only to Gideon. A fast talker, the doctor was! But none of the Hippies were impressed. The law students knew the law, and they understood what was going on. They were undesirables in the area, and this was a cover up. Clearly a cover up! But they didn't really care. Nothing could give Holy Joe back to them. So let the doctor handle matters in his own way. For now anyway! Their time would come! And they already knew what they would do!

Thinking that the fatality had been one of the Hippies at the Commune, the doctor listened to Gideon. Gideon told him the accident had claimed a beloved brother, and if the doctor would notify the officials according to law, the Commune would cause no trouble. There was great sadness, Gideon said, and it would be a benefit to close this case, and its sorrow as soon as possible. It was no surprise that the doctor quickly agreed. He seemed vastly relieved, and assured the young men that none of them had to be further contacted. The information provided by Gideon was all he would need, he said, to settle matters in town. The doctor prepared the requested forms and a necessary letter for interment. And that's what the intent of the Hippies was!

The doctor had expressed his condolences before leaving the Commune. He did not mention his son, but the young men no longer cared! It was over! They didn't know or care either just how or whether the doctor would notify anyone else. They had told the doctor that it was important to them to bury their adored brother in private. The doctor, of course, understood this, too!

A short item in the morning paper really said very little. It just noted that a resident of the Commune had passed on, and was apparently due to an accident. A funeral was pending! The son of the doctor was not mentioned. The Hippies knew this was only a network of police and small town politicians looking out for one another. They also knew it was a conspiracy, and if they had made the decision to bring in high-powered lawyers from their family firms, the town would suffer. The misassumptions, and the sloppiness of the elected "ins", a few political czars, too, would better the young men's plans. Lots of work to do! Holy Joe would not be forgotten! A reminder would forever be visible! The opportunity had virtually been a gift, and the young men had not lied once about anything!

Armed with the certificate from the doctor, Gideon, Moses and Gabriel went to the mortuary to purchase a fine and expensive coffin. The best you have! A bronze will do, and thank you for your help! And no, they chose to handle the preparations themselves. But thank you anyway! And no, they could manage the coffin on their cart. Thanks again!

With this done, while Gabriel drove back to the Commune, Gideon and Moses, with plenty of cash from Western Union visited the local cemetery. Four lots were purchased. The grave would be in the center of this huge plot, and with a low brick wall around the collective space, they told the caretaker. There would also be a large marble monument. There was still more to do! And to the florist they went! The order of thirty dozen red and white roses caused nearly a panic in the small shop. This was unheard of! The florist, with a bonus already in hand, called airlines and a market out of state. The order arrived on time! Thank you kindly, they said.

The townspeople had never seen such splendid preparations for a funeral. A nice, but puzzling event, and they had made plans to attend to show the young men they understood their pain. It was so sad, they said. The townspeople had had very little to do with the Commune all along, but, they reasoned, it is a neighborly thing to be supportive when sadness comes. Of course, they did not know Holy Joe, or even much about anything pertaining to the accident. That wasn't the main topic of the day, however! The funeral was! But nobody knew the biggest secret in town, and it had to do with the funeral! No one knew it but those who had loved Holy Joe. And they were not talking!

Back at the Commune, with pain they could hardly handle, the Hippies gently placed their precious little bundle of love in the great bronze coffin. Along side were the balls, frisbees and stuffed animals. They tied Holy Joe's bandana around his neck, and then each one kissed and stroked him. They wept and prayed, and comforted one another. After their good-byes, they sealed the coffin, and stayed beside it all night long!

It was a strange, but grand funeral procession that left the Commune early the next day. Holy Joe's little wagon was filled with white roses and pulled along by Jacob. He walked a few yards ahead of Gideon who was praying quietly with his Bible open. Next came the cart bearing the coffin with one spray of mixed roses laying on its burnished surface. The mule looked fittingly sad with a garland of red roses around his head. Gabriel walked along side. The twelve remaining young men followed in groups of three. Other than their sadness, they were all their usual selves in both dress and behavior. It was not a show they were putting on. Only love and honor was being expressed by those who were so deeply hurt!

The townspeople lined the street to watch the cortege, and when it passed, they followed it to the cemetery. The Hippies did not mind this if they were there to mourn. And indeed, when they saw the grief with the tears and dazed expressions of the young men, the good people of the town did mourn! It was a grief that they knew was real! So they stayed for the services, and wept with the young men, whose good-bye to their brother was heartwrenching! The people didn't seem to think it was odd at all that none of the family members of the deceased were present. They only said how nice it was that the young men had decided to bury their brother where he had fallen!

The townspeople stood all afternoon in the hot sun while the eulogies were given. Fifteen in all! Each young man tearfully said his piece, and the coffin was lowered. Two dozen white roses were dropped into the grave, and still the services continued! Hosea and Amos sang more hymns, more poems were read, and more scriptures were quoted. Hosea finally sang the closing hymn, Amazing Grace, and Gideon gave the benediction while the others held hands and prayed along with him. The funeral was over! It had lasted five hours! And it was a beautiful good-bye, too! Every one was spent, but there was not a dry eye any where! Beautiful, but just emotionally draining, said those who had attended!

Many people offered to prepare food for the tired and brokenhearted mourners, but they declined. Thank you very much, they said. With hearts so heavy that they could hardly carry them, the young men drove back to the Commune in their cart.

No supper that night. No one wanted to eat. No one wanted to talk. Most of them sat around the rickety table with heads bowed. A rustling movement drew their attention to Jacob who was going through his old college backpack. Removing a law textbook, he placed it on the table gazing quietly at its cover. No one said anything. They all knew it was time, though!

Time to finish up here. Time to arrange for the monument. Time to remind those in charge that the low brick enclosure for Holy Joe's plot would be a priority structure. Time to order one dozen roses to be delivered every Sunday to the plot. Time to get enrolled for the fall semester at their respective universities. Yes, it was time!

But tonight they had to rest! There was one more thing they had to do this day, though. Before getting into their sleeping bags, the young men knew they must decide what inscription was to be chiseled on Holy Joe's monument. This would be simple, but elegant, and most appropriate! It would be truthful, and speak their own hearts, too! Hosea was a fine artist as well as having a fine singing voice, so he prepared a sample drawing for their inspection.

HOLY JOE

JULY 16, 1967

OUR LITTLE BROTHER

GREATER LOVE?

WE THINK NOT!

It was very appropriate, and they were pleased. It spoke their hearts! Now it was time to rest. Tomorrow would come!

The next day, the monument, as well as the brick wall, was ordered. All of this, the young men said, was only the tribute that Holy Joe deserved. There were some fine markers in the cemetery for the town's wealthiest and most important citizens, but none would be as splendid as what they planned for Holy Joe. They would have to wait for a few more days, though.

The Hippies didn't think much about their place in the universe now. They didn't follow their religion either. A change had occurred with their sorrow, and they knew why! Holy Joe was still leading them toward the light, and was watching out for them, too! More than ever, they knew what they must do; get on with their lives, get back in their universities. And close their Commune! They could see things better now. Holy Joe had done this for them. They could never stop weeping, though!

In just a few days the monument was completed, but the masonry work took a while longer. When all was ready to be inspected, the young men were truly at a loss for words! Both structures were magnificent! Only bottomless purses at work could produce such splendor, they told each other, but they were so very pleased! The inscription on the monument was clearly defined. And reading it over and over, the young men cried. In their hearts, though, they also had to believe that Holy Joe wasn't really there any more, but he was happy somewhere else! Maybe somewhere they could not know. But somewhere special! Somewhere nice! Somewhere!

Yes, Holy Joe was somewhere! Somewhere special! Somewhere nice, too! He was happy! And as his friends on Earth were speaking, Holy Joe was aboard The Big White Eagle who had just landed in Canine Heaven. The Great Collie, knowing that Holy Joe would be the new Religious Leader of Canine Heaven, asked Wrangler and O'Casey to greet Holy Joe when he arrived. And very soon now, he would be shaking paws with the two canines, and getting acquainted here!

Holy Joe knew nothing of the honors bestowed on him when he left Earth. He knew nothing of the sorrow. And he was never to know any of the events of his last four months on Earth. It had been written in The Great Charter of Canine Heaven, that such information was valueless for the well-being of residents of Canine Heaven. But Holy Joe was not thinking about the charter today. That would come later! In fact, he was not thinking much about Earth either! His memories would always be with him, and they were so very important. He could see, though, that his new position was very important. They had told him that at the Briefing Center. So he couldn't be distracted right now with anything!

Yes, Holy Joe would be busy! Plenty busy! First, after the initial greeting, he would meet with The Great Collie, and be officially welcomed to Canine Heaven. Canine Heaven! And Earth?

Well, Earth was quite far away, and seeming more distant all the time! But Holy Joe had only just arrived here! A little homesick? If so, he had no time to yield to it! Besides, from what he had seen and heard thus far, it looked as if his afterlife might be as interesting as his time on Earth! If that's the case, there will be no complaints! Holy Joe smiled as he straightened his bandana. He was already happy here in Canine Heaven! And Holy Joe had smiled as he saluted The Big White Eagle, and he continued to smile as he stepped to grasp the waving outstretched paws of Wrangler and O'Casey. Holy Joe had arrived in Canine Heaven! And events had progressed elsewhere as well.

On Earth, though sad, the young men were coming to terms and helping themselves. The Commune closed! Good-byes, and promises to keep in touch had been tearfully said. It was not easy! They had gone through a lot together in the last three years, and most especially, this past week. Their goal to find the universal meaning of life had not been reached. But they knew also, that good things had happened in their quest. It had brought them together in a perfect relationship for their purposes. And, of course, it had brought Holy Joe! So they had not really failed! Maybe all of them collectively had been the soul of the Commune with their harmony, but Holy Joe was its heart! No need to recap any further! It's time to go!

Private and corporate aircraft flew in and out of the town's tiny airfield for most of the morning. Gideon stayed behind for another day. His own family jet would be here tomorrow. There were a few things he wanted to take care of at the Commune anyway. And he waved to his comrades as their jets roared away with family and corporate icons emblazoned on the sides. The parents of the young men had seen them through both a happy and a sad experience. Now it was time to bring them home, and the families sent their wealth to do it. This is the way it will be from now on, and maybe it is fitting, Gideon was thinking as he returned to the Commune. He stopped by the cemetery on his way and told Holy Joe about it!

Before leaving the next day, Gideon gave the hutch of rabbits and the mule to a nearby farm. It was to the same farmer who had leased the two acres of lake property to the Hippies for their Commune, and had suffered the anger of his neighbors for doing so. But he had kept his word. He was happy to get the free animals, too! Gideon shook hands, and told the farmer that he would come back some day just to see the place again. He would be very welcome!

And it was Gideon who returned from the corporate world first. It had been three years. He was a Junior Executive in the family law firm now, and it was a suit and tie job, too! He brought along his young wife to see the Commune site. First, though, they visited Holy Joe's plot at the cemetery. The splendor of the site was still awesome! The beautiful and polished marble monument stood like a lovely centerpiece in the cemetery. Gideon and his wife read the inscription aloud together and wept. A most impressive farewell this was, and Holy Joe must have been special indeed to deserve this magnificence! The young wife held her husband's hand and wept.

At the Commune site, they found the table and the cart trashed. Everywhere was thick with weeds and briers, but a white rose bush, now wild and stringy, still bloomed profusely. Gideon showed his wife where the tents were; where a fire was made; where the rickety table was; where the rabbit hutch was built; where the mule grazed, and how well it was organized at the Commune. She was very impressed with such efficiency of The Corporation, as she playfully said the Commune resembled. And then Gideon spotted a well-chewed ball laying near the rose bush!

Gideon began weeping as he held the ball to his face with both hands. His wife tried to comfort him, but she was puzzled, too! A ball causing this distress? She had forgotten about the dog that Gideon had often mentioned in his letters, and she did not remember what its name was either. Until now! Saying nothing, but knowing and understanding so well, the young wife gently led her husband away.

Meanwhile, Holy Joe had done a fine job in Canine Heaven. He was the Chaplain, and a better choice was not possible considering Holy Joe's education level. What he had learned in the Commune was serving him well! His knowledge of philosophy, science, religion, law and literature was helpful in much problem solving for the residents, and they all needed help at times. He was always there for them, too!

Yes, Holy Joe's afterlife was good! And his memories were good, too! Often thinking of his days on Earth with his Hippy pals, Holy Joe would chuckle. He knew that he had served them well, but they had served him well also! It was all about need! And love! He had loved and needed them. They loved and needed him! It was great! Just great! Thank you, Canis Major!

This morning in Chapel, as Holy Joe waited to step to the podium, he could not help but notice O'Casey's friendly demeanor. Now this was very unlike The Editor of The Canine Weekly. While he was, by nature, not a charming canine, O'Casey had also appeared sad for several weeks now. But today, he was all smiles, and greeting everyone. And it was sure nice to see! Holy Joe knew about O'Casey's meeting with His Greatness yesterday, but he didn't know the nature of it. Maybe something good, he mused. Maybe something good!

Holy Joe gave O'Casey no more time, but Jetaway stayed in his thoughts. He so wanted to see Jetaway, and at least to comfort him. Canis Major, please!

Just before Holy Joe began to speak to the worshipers, he silently offered thanks for the goodness in Canine Heaven. And he gave thanks, too, for all the goodness on Earth. It was there in the Commune where he had first learned compassion and caring! Holy Joe prayed that Jetaway would find peace, and his burden lifted. And he gave very special thanks for O'Casey's happy smile!

Holy Joe caught Carolyn's eye for a brief moment, and he quickly offered a short prayer just for her.

"The position! The position of Most Private Secretary to The Great Collie, Canis Major, for Carolyn!"

Holy Joe stepped to the podium.

The Great Collie would not take his usual place of honor in the Chapel today. The meeting with Jetaway would be consuming most of his morning. Already advised, Holy Joe began:

"Good morning, my dear Brothers and Sisters! I welcome you ...

THE GREAT COLLIE'S
BUSY WEEK

The Great Collie would miss the joy of Chapel this day. His only appointment was with Jetaway. And due to the nature of the summons, this would be a lengthy meeting. He had instructed his secretary to schedule nothing more!

After going over Jetaway's personal file as well as the files of Jetaway's Canine Heaven Connections, there would be time for a short nap before Jetaway was expected. He had a busy week, and it wasn't over yet! He waited for Jetaway to make his appearance, and mused about his several meetings so far this week. Yesterday, it had been a meeting with O'Casey and Lolita, and more sessions the day before with King, George and Hildegard. All of these talks were productive, and His Greatness was most satisfied with each outcome. But the reunion between O'Casey and Little Ben was perhaps the happiest!

Lolita, the beautiful Afghan Director of the Puppy Compound, was ordered to the Big Bone Palace, and the puppy, Little Ben, was to accompany her. Also summoned to appear was O'Casey, and at the same hour as Lolita. O'Casey was a bit puzzled to see Lolita until he saw Little Ben frisking about. Choosing to not greet the other, they stood quietly waiting for The Great Collie to address them. His Greatness had gone immediately to the point of having these two, O'Casey and Lolita, appear before him! And he minced no words!

"O'Casey, it is time for you to get to know your little brother again. You will be able to see Little Ben more in the coming weeks to play and to get on with your afterlives as a family. You make your relationship known! You may now take Little Ben outside for a romp on the Palace grounds. When I call, I will talk to you further."

O'Casey was so delighted he had almost cried. When he and Little Ben had departed, The Great Collie addressed a stoic Lolita! He minced no words there either! This time he was angry!

"Sometimes you have to bend a mite, Lolita." He told her sternly. "We know how you love, and protect the puppies, too! You do a fine job at the Compound as its Director, Lolita. But you never had babies of your own, so you may not fully understand a real blood kinship. And this is the first one we are aware of in Canine Heaven, so we had to bend and meet it head on! That's leadership at its finest, Lolita. I know O'Casey, and I know it is somewhat justified to be arrogant with him. But you shut him out completely, Lolita! I want you to see that this was family, real family, and you refused to recognize it!"

"Sir, these puppies are like my own babies! As you know, I was deprived of giving birth by a vicious attack on my sister and me by a crazed drug addict. My sister, as well as my Master, could not survive. So, Your Greatness, I see these puppies here in Canine Heaven as my babies, and my family, too!" Lolita had said with great feeling.

"I know all that, my dear, and I am very sorry." The Great Collie told her in a more gentle tone. "Your record as it is in our files, documents the sadness you experienced on Earth, Lolita, and your records were well-researched, too, before appointing you Director of the Puppy Compound, or Puppy Community if you wish. Lolita, Dear Child, we know your sorrow, and we know your superb ability as well. You are the best choice I could have made for this very important position, and usually we are pleased. Only the matter of O'Casey is causing my displeasure, Lolita. I care not whether you and O'Casey are bitter enemies, or you are happy friends. It is hardly the issue here. O'Casey and Little Ben must be given more time together. I suggest that you do not curtail it any further! Without good reason, of course. Lolita, I know you are in charge, and this will not cause any change in your duties. This was an unusual case, and now we know how a family situation must be handled from now on. And we can still love the puppies! Enough said, Lolita?"

"Yes, Sir, we can still love them." Lolita smiled. "And we do!"

"And, Lolita," The Great Collie was smiling, too! "Please retrieve Little Ben from his play with O'Casey, and do remind O'Casey to come to my office at once. You are excused, Lolita."

"Thank you, Sir!" Lolita had smiled again, and sweetly so, as she departed The Great Collie's presence.

The Great Collie knew that this canine would continue taking care of her appointed position in the same way she always had. Lolita was bossy and arrogant, but that was just being herself! Lolita could be a dog-goned pain! And she was most of the time! Her love and concern for the puppies more than made up for her superego, though. Well, it helped anyway! The Great Collie smiled and decided that these two, Lolita and O'Casey, were very much alike in their ways! He also knew that the Little Ben problem was happily solved, and Lolita would not unduly interfere any longer. O'Casey would do right, too! Or else!

When O'Casey returned after handing Little Ben back to Lolita's authority, he was one happy Irish Wolf Hound!

"I thank you, Sir. I thank you!" He had said still smiling broadly.

"You are welcome, O'Casey, and I am sure you will be reasonable in the new relationship with your little brother. Yes?"

"Yes, Sir, I will be! I will be!"

"Thank you, O'Casey." The Great One said warmly. "And now there are a few, but important, matters that I will decide with your help."

"Yes, Sir?"

"First, as you know, The Yearly Report will appear in tomorrow's edition of The Canine Weekly. And that is fine and proper, but there will be some extra news items from my office that are to be published also. Are you following me O'Casey?"

"Yes, Sir!"

"Alright! The newspaper will be set tomorrow as usual, but it won't be apportioned until the next day! Alright? The special news from my office, given only to you, will be handled completely by you, O'Casey, and not Durkin, or Buddy either. They are talkative! Now, are you still following me?"

"I understand, Sir. I understand!"

"Thank you, O'Casey. Here, you will find the materials in this folder with special instructions. If you need further clarification, please contact The Chief of Staff. Well, you know who!"

"Yes, Sir, I know Wrangler," smiled O'Casey. "And the integrity of the office of The Great Collie will be served, Your Honor!"

The Great Collie usually issued his official messages, and had them delivered by the Message Center. This issue was different, though! Yes, the Canine Weekly would better serve his purpose. The Great Collie intended to make some important announcements of interest to all Canine Heaven residents. He wanted them to be informed of his action, and at about the same time. Everyone read the Canine Weekly, and delaying it for one day would do just fine. They would understand! Besides, His Greatness had another idea that he knew would simply delight Canine Heaven's population. He hadn't fully worked it out yet, but he hoped it could come to pass. He was so busy, though! He could not remember a week that had been so demanding of his time!

Now, resting and thinking and waiting for Jetaway, The Great Collie read his notes again. He smiled when he recalled O'Casey's dismay about what the residents were to be told when the Canine Weekly was delayed. They did enjoy their newspaper every Saturday!

"O'Casey, we are a truthful society here in Canine Heaven. The only explanation necessary is the truth, and the truth is simply that the Canine Weekly will be delayed for one day only. This is by order of The Great Collie."

"Yes, Sir." O'Casey had answered as he put the sealed folder in his pouch. "Is that all, Your Greatness?"

"Well, I am mulling over an idea! I don't know yet if I can manage it, and there's no need to discuss it now. But while you are here, I do want to speak of a certain burden that is causing an unnecessary amount of pain for you! It doesn't matter how it came to my desk. You are, of course, aware of that burden, O'Casey, and you must not concern yourself any longer with this painful, and debilitating feeling that you maybe offended your breed, the Irish Wolf Hound, while on Earth.

"The incident involving this human, O'Banion, must be laid to rest. I have spoken to O'Grady, the patriarch of an illustrious breed, your breed! O'Grady resides in the Senior Community, and I am assured that in a situation such as yours can be forgiven, and understood, too! O'Grady says the Irish Wolf Hound is an affable and caring breed, but it is in their nature to take care of one another. And in your youth, that's all you tried to do, O'Casey. It was not a laudable response, but understandable. Your breed is not shamed! This was not a minor crime on O'Banion's part. Simply dastardly! Your ancestors may even be proud of you, O'Casey. In any case, you are not in Canine Heaven to grieve over Earthly events. You are here because of good service, and that speaks volumes! Now enjoy your reward. I know I should have spoken about this before now, O'Casey. Please forgive me! And I see you are happy today. Yes?" Extending his paw, The Great Collie smiled.

"Yes, Sir, I am happy today! And it is because you have helped me twice. I am most grateful, Your Honor." O'Casey had said sincerely. "But I do have one question about Little Ben, Sir."

"You are most welcome, O'Casey, for any help I could offer. What question do you have?"

"How did you know about Little Ben? I told no one."

"Madeline, Lolita's assistant, told Wrangler, who brought the matter to my attention. You are excused, O'Casey."

When O'Casey made his departure, he was in a happy, happy state! The Great Collie had smiled to see this. He knew that it was time to help this arrogant opinionated canine a bit. O'Casey was still O'Casey, though! But he had had a great burden lifted, and a happy solution to another problem. His Greatness was most pleased!

The day before tackling the O'Casey and Lolita feud, The Great Collie successfully handled matters with George, King and Hildegard. All three had been summoned to The Big Bone Palace. Dealing with the egotistical Hildegard was always a sticky problem. She was first on his list!

How to use Hildegard's talents, and to curb her impulses at the same time, was a task that The Great Collie never enjoyed thinking about. Why Hildegard did not involve herself more with other Seniors was beyond all reason, too! The nice Senior Community was a lively and interesting part of Canine Heaven. The Seniors always had something going on for their enjoyment. They organized tours to visit the Museum, or to go to the Theater or stroll around in Fleecy Park. There was lots to do!

The Seniors enjoyed service and respect. No real duties were assigned to them. Their meals were often delivered to them. Holy Joe visited a lot. Oddly enough, Lolita welcomed the Seniors to see the puppies at play. The choir was often there. The quartet arranged many special programs just for the Seniors. O'Casey gave some of his best lectures at the Community, and picnics and parties were frequently organized for its residents as well. It was a happy afterlife experience for most of the old canines. But not quite all! Hildegard took little notice of their retirement joys, and left the Community every day to spend time in the Village. Particularly around the Palace!

Hildegard was a nuisance at The Big Bone Palace. She bothered the Whippets as they worked by offering her DRAWING room expertise as a guide to what they were doing. Hildegard, a French Poodle of Superb Cultural Experience, Dear Ones, always had solutions! Just ask! Paris, London and New York, Darlings! A great, great heritage, Dears! It was an aggravation to the Whippets, and a big one at that! They could not be disrespectful to Hildegard. Not to a Senior Resident of Canine Heaven! So, in desperation, the Whippets took their case directly to Wrangler, Staff Chief. The Great Collie was immediately advised!

Since certain changes were going to be made at the Palace anyway, maybe it was time to relocate

Hildegard's energies! The Great Collie devised a plan, and then he summoned Hildegard. Thinking about it now, he smiled at how the plan had worked so successfully!

When Hildegard hurried to meet with His Greatness, she had assumed that he expected something very important from her. It would be an honor to serve The Great Collie. And only she could do an excellent job, of course!

"The Great Collie needs some quality advice, and I'm sure I can deliver! With my special experiences in London, New York and Paris, I can help!" Hildegard had gushed to herself while she waited for The Great Collie to address her. "I can do it, Your Honor! I can!"

When he had spoken of his plans for her, Hildegard was a bit disappointed. It wasn't quite what she had expected, but she was most gracious as she heard what His Greatness had in mind. And he had spoken his mind! Clearly! He told Hildegard that henceforth, she was assigned to the Chapel. She would assist Holy Joe in any manner that HE saw fit to conduct Chapel business! His Greatness expected a superb use of her many talents! Now, don't disappoint!

Upon hearing this praise, Hildegard had gushed some more, and began to explain to The Great Collie what changes needed to be made at the Chapel. There could be a more splendid activity from the choir; more professionalism in the quartet, and Holy Joe's posture at the podium could be improved! Just so many things to be done, and Hildegard would do them all! Holy Joe must be delighted! Thank you, Your Honor! Holy Joe is enthusiastically giving thanks, too!

Well, Holy Joe didn't quite know about it yet! His Greatness was certain that Holy Joe could manage Hildegard's disruptive behavior better than anyone else. The rest of Canine Heaven's population, as well as the Whippets, were clearly tired of Hildegard's meddling, and her snootiness, too. Yes, Holy Joe could handle Hildegard! Holy Joe had a lot of patience, and that patience, no doubt, would be tested every day! But, it would work out! His Greatness sent Hildegard on her way, and gave his attention to George. He would explain to Holy Joe later! And he had not spent a lot of time with George either. Only a few minutes!

George, a St. Bernard, is from Alps Country. That's what he calls the huge mountain range in Switzerland where he worked with his Master in a Search and Rescue Operation. George was summoned by The Great Collie because of his argument with the Malemutes and Huskies. George bragged to them about the great rescues he had made, and how many sick and lost travelers he had saved in his work. The Eskimo Canines had done rescue service, too. They knew the danger in the Arctic Circle where they slaved to help those in need. The Alpine Region was tame in comparison! And mostly they ignored George, but he kept on needling them with his tall tales. The Eskimo Canines complained to Wrangler. And George was summoned!

The Great Collie had had little experience in dealing with a heckler, he told George, and it didn't matter how, or where, George plied his trade. This was harassment! It would not be tolerated! Who was better at survival methods was not important here. But it was reasonable for the Eskimo Canines, after hearing George's diatribe over and over, to believe their own frozen tundra to be the more difficult region in which to struggle with rescue efforts! The Great Collie agreed, and had spoken some more to George!

Those canines, George was told, had done a responsible job in their duties in Canine Heaven. A lot more could be said of their performance! They didn't boast or needle either, and you are to tone down your rhetoric, George! This behavior will stop right now! And then The Great Collie had told George as an afterthought, that his breed, the fine St. Bernard, would expect more of him. That did the trick! George promised to apologize to the Eskimo Canines and he had said that he would have a talk also with Holy Joe. His Greatness smiled warmly, and shook the extended paw. He then had patted George on the shoulder as he excused him!

King was handled just as quickly as George had been. His Greatness advised King to stop threatening the residents of Canine Heaven by teasing them about his strong and powerful physique. Even though the other canines knew it was a fun thing for King, it was still a bit intimidating, The Great Collie said. A friendly Rottweiler, King was, and one of the most popular canines here. So a more totally shocked canine was not to be found in Canine Heaven than King as he heard the reason for his summons.

King was just so sorry, he had told The Great Collie, that he had been the cause of unrest among the inhabitants! He was so very sorry that the flexing, and showing off his muscles, was badly misunderstood. King had said this was really only a joke between him and the also muscular O'Casey. Being the largest breed in Canine Heaven, King said, O'Casey, The Irish Wolf Hound, was also very proud of his strength. So the two of them made jokes about who could "paddle" the other. Everyone seemed to know this, and King could not, for the life of him, imagine who would find it offensive! O'Casey would not complain. So, who did?

The Great Collie had told King that it didn't really matter who had called this to Wrangler's attention. They had to check these things out! Even though His Greatness knew of the ugly editorial that O'Casey had written about The Rottweilers, he also knew that King, a truthful canine, was stating the facts of his relationship with O'Casey. And His Greatness decided that maybe those two canines were not pals, but respect was certainly there! Besides, no other canines had really been at risk! This complaint was frivolous, and unfair!

The Great Collie had told King that his summons was a mistake, and he felt badly that it had come to pass! And no minutes of this meeting would find its way into King's private records. After thanking His Greatness, King shook his paw, and Wrangler's, too! Before being excused, however; King was still talking about, and wondering who his enemy was! Who didn't like him? Wrangler and The Great Collie had both laughed, and almost together they told King that he could probably find the answer in London, or maybe Paris! But they couldn't say for sure! Their lips were sealed! King had laughed along with them. They liked King. Everyone else liked King, too. Well, almost everyone! But, just like on Earth, the troublemakers had a "field day" in Canine Heaven as well!

"Well," The Great Collie was thinking as he came out of his reverie, "It is time for Jetaway now, and I believe he is entering with Wrangler. Yes, he is here!"

His Greatness saw Jetaway's unhappy state right away, and thought he might be upset about something else, for The Great Collie had yet to address him! A sad sight Jetaway was, too. His Greatness immediately took control!

"Wrangler, please leave us alone. I will call you if I need you."

"Yes, Sir, but first, I have information you will be interested to know, Your Greatness, when you speak to this canine. May I continue?"

"Yes, Wrangler, please! I do want a bowl of water brought first, though."

"Yes, Sir, I will ring for it now."

"Thank you, Wrangler. Jetaway, here have a refreshing drink of water. Now, now, my boy, be calm and..."

"Yes, yes, Sir, I ... I... don't know, know...," blubbered Jetaway.

"Let's hear what Wrangler will tell us, my son. We will try to fix what is wrong!" said The Great Collie gently.

"Thank you, Sir," Wrangler said. "I talked with Jetaway just last week. He confided to me that the Canine Weekly, you know their Press Pigeon Service is unreliable at times, and I fear one of its releases has caused much pain. You see, Sir, this news was passed to Jetaway by one of the Canine Weekly's employees. It should not have been! Sir, as I told you, this news was very disturbing to Jetaway, for he has a wing-loss situation and was unable to alert his Connections about a problem on the Earth which I now know, Sir, has sadly been misunderstood!"

"We must talk with O'Casey. I don't like it, Wrangler! This Pigeon Service running rampant! It must be controlled more responsibly! I'm sure O'Casey was unaware of this breach, though!" said The Great Collie angrily as he tenderly held Jetaway's paw.

"Yes, Sir, O'Casey was unaware that Buddy had rushed to tell Jetaway of an impending arrival in Canine Heaven. He told Jetaway that it was a family member, and his Connections would need to know. Well, Sir, Jetaway was unable to alert anyone! His wing-loss prevented this communication. Jetaway knew there would need to be preparations made for the potential arrival if it should occur. I did not fully understand what I was hearing at the time, for I did not know of any arrival until yesterday. I understand perfectly now just what has happened! And, Your Greatness, this is not all!

"Jetaway is grieving for his family on Earth as he believes they are quite sad, and grieving, too. Jetaway is also concerned because it is family, and he feels he is needed here as well. He feels helpless, Your Greatness! And in addition to the worries of the humans, and his duties to his Connections as a loyal canine, Jetaway is simply devastated and overwhelmed! He is worried, too, because he doesn't understand the nature of his summons, Sir. These concerns have upset Jetaway greatly. Now, as you recall, when we researched this canine's file, as well as those of his Canine Heaven Connections, we found no negative information. Nothing unusual! All rather routine! I believe you will find some benefit in what I have said, Your Greatness. I will be in my office if you need me." Wrangler concluded as he prepared to depart.

"Thank you, Wrangler, you have been a great help. Please stay, and we will work through this problem with Jetaway together. All three of us! He has misunderstood the news item, but it was a garbled and unclear message, and never should have been delivered. O'Casey is going to hang that Bloodhound, Durkin, or was it Buddy, out to dry! Overstepping authority! But let O'Casey handle that! Now, now, Jetaway, you must stay calm so you can help us! You are needlessly worrying yourself! I have some news for you, and you will need to get in touch with your Connections. A newcomer is arriving, and ..."

"Then, my human family is grieving! That makes me sad! And the notices for a pending arrival are done through the Message Center," sobbed Jetaway. "And I don ... don't know why I am here, Your Greatness."

"You are here, Jetaway, because you were summoned to be here. You are not here for any reason beyond this matter on which I shall advise you. Wrangler, please get Jetaway another bowl of water, and get one for me, too!"

"Yes, Sir," said Wrangler as he refilled Jetaway's bowl, and also poured one for The Great Collie. Wrangler decided that he himself could use a bowl of fresh water as well! He sipped and waited for His Greatness to speak.

"My dear boy," he began, "I can see your stress more clearly now. This information was not channeled in the way we usually provide it, and this change in procedure caused you to worry. You could not know that the new arrival is perhaps a special case. Well, he is a special newcomer! He has been employed at the Briefing Center for ten years."

"Then ... then, who?" asked Jetaway.

"Now, I will get to that in time. I think it is important for you to fully understand just how these things work. The newcomer's time at the Center will be over as of today, and he will be in Canine Heaven tomorrow at noon.

"You see, he was given a choice, as all canines are, of being useful where he was or coming directly here when he left Earth. Being a coddled canine, he wanted the same treatment whatever the situation or circumstances. And at the Briefing Center, he found a happy companionship with those in charge. Very, very compatible! It was fortunate for him that they needed a page, or maybe, they just wanted him to stay with them at the Center. He liked the idea! Not much work; very little dedication, and plenty of catering and attention. His employers, I am told, did more for him than he ever did for them. They didn't mind, and he certainly was happy about the whole set-up!

"But, he could only stay there, you see, for ten years. He is arriving tomorrow, and you, Jetaway, happen to be one Connection! The news delivered to you was incorrect. You understood this arrival as a current happening, and it was not! You wanted to alert your Connections to prepare for what looked to you like an emergency. And it was kind of like that, too. But, you could not. Your restrictions prevented you from a responsible handling of family affairs as you understood it. Now, do you read me, Jetaway?" The Great Collie asked.

"I think so, Sir." Jetaway replied. He was feeling better now. He was here because of the newcomer, and not for a reprimand. That was good to know, but, why was The Great Collie talking about this to him? Why not Buster? Or Rover? Or even The Old Black Dog? Any one of them could arrange the welcome for the new arrival. With his restrictions, it was not possible for Jetaway to do any planning, and he began to worry again. He felt helpless again, too. There was so much to be done, and tomorrow would come too soon! The Great Collie was aware of the restrictive nature of this situation. He had said so! Then, why? Jetaway didn't know. He listened carefully as The Great Collie continued to address him.

"Jetaway, your wing-loss suspension has been lifted by my special order. I have your wings here. You are now prepared to alert your Connections that a new member of your Canine Heaven family is arriving tomorrow at noon. May I suggest, too, that you be more careful to avoid wing-loss in the future. Now, fun is fun, and Napoleon is Napoleon!

"Napoleon is a good Constable. Just overly alert, that's all. So, you must snicker behind his back! Especially in Chapel!"

The Great Collie was teasing a mite with Jetaway. That sad, frightened and worried canine had clearly calmed himself now that he understood. He smiled as he promised to be more careful when Napoleon was around. His Greatness was pleased, but he still had something to say!

Jetaway needed a little pep talk on a couple of other matters.

"You have been most kind, Sir. I do appreciate your help so much, and I do know what I must accomplish on a short notice. We'll be ready for the arrival at noon tomorrow as scheduled. I thank you again." Jetaway said sincerely.

"You are welcome," smiled The Great Collie. "But I have not quite finished with you!"

"Yes, Sir?" Jetaway asked as he began to unpack his wings which Wrangler had brought to The Great Collie's desk as instructed.

"Well," His Greatness smiled, but a hint of urgency was in his voice, too. "We can do nothing to ease human grief on Earth. That, as well as other Earth related problems are their own to deal with as they choose. We do not address these matters in Canine Heaven. We do, however, remember with love those that we served, and the humans who loved us as well. But, Jetaway, we can do absolutely nothing more! We can not make a priority of dealing with Earthly frustrations. We are far beyond that! Now, we are sustained with our love and our memories. I suspect the Earthlings are the same. Do you follow me, Jetaway?"

The Great Collie reached out again, and took Jetaway's paw. He liked this caring and responsible Spaniel! Gazing intently into the canine's tired face, His Greatness said softly, "You are an uncommon worrywart!"

"I understand, Sir, and I know what you say is true. I do fret more than I should I guess, but I just didn't know why I had been summoned. I felt maybe that I had displeased you by losing my wings again. I know now you would not concern yourself with that, Sir. I can prepare for the newcomer as you expect of me. I don't know him, but I do know a lot about him. Buster knew him! They shared the same household on Earth. My previous household, too, Sir, and I do love him very much. He is family! Now, he may be spoiled, but he is family! I love him, Sir, and the others will also!" Jetaway said earnestly.

"We will all love him," smiled The Great Collie. "I have a surprise which I think he will enjoy when I extend my welcome to him tomorrow."

"You do?" exclaimed Jetaway. "May I ask what the surprise is, Sir?"

"Yes, you may! First, though, there is one other item that I want to touch on involving your situation, and it is this; when you become overwhelmed with burdens that seem to have no solution, I want you to contact Wrangler, who in turn, will arrange a meeting with me," said The Great Collie as he helped the struggling Jetaway with his wings.

"Yes, Sir, I will! I promise!"

"Very well. This whole affair was a mistake from the start. But, I am here for those times of unrest. You understand now, don't you, Jetaway?"

"Yes, Sir, I do understand! It was, you know, family business, and I ought to handle it myself, and ..."

"Well, your sorrows are our sorrows as well! Right, Wrangler?"

"Absolutely, Sir!" Wrangler agreed.

"Alright, now we all agree," smiled His Greatness snapping the last buckle shut on Jetaway's wings.

"And I was about to tell you what surprise awaited your new Connection, Jetaway. Well, he is going to be my personal Office Boy! Now, how about that for a welcome?"

"If there isn't too much work, Sir, I am sure he will do just fine. I hear that he's got an ego that won't quit!" laughed Jetaway thinking of the antics of the newcomer to exert control where it was needed for his comfort! Buster knew all about it. He was there!

Wrangler had been called to a meeting in the Council Chambers, and Jetaway was left alone with The Great Collie who had not yet excused him. Today was the first time Jetaway had been to The Big Bone Palace since his own welcome to Canine Heaven a few years earlier. He felt very honored to be here, too! His Greatness had treated him and his concerns so kindly along with good counsel and advice. This was an honor!

Jetaway had never expected the care and good will that he had received. He had been so worried and upset, he just didn't know what he had expected. Certainly nothing like this! Jetaway did not pause to think that it was his own compassionate and responsible behavior that had impressed The Great Collie as well as Wrangler. They wanted to help, and they HAD helped! His Greatness had even helped Jetaway strap on his wings in a loving gesture. And, in addition, His Greatness had actually confided an important Palace appointment. Jetaway was puzzled, but grateful, and he knew he was enjoying himself here. He knew, too, that he should be leaving the Big Bone Palace to prepare for the arrival of the newcomer. And he had yet to allow that he was excused!

While he waited, Jetaway, listening to The Great Collie's jokes, noticed a pretty new coral shell desk with Carolyn's name imprinted in gold on a silver inlay. Wow!

"Forgive me, Sir," said Jetaway, "I wonder if that pretty new desk means a pretty Black Labrador will use it."

"You are correct in your assumption of an important appointment, Jetaway," said His Greatness with a smile. "She will begin her duties in a day or two. Carolyn's title? The Most Private Secretary to The Great Collie! She is yet to be advised. I trust you will keep a secret?"

"I will, Sir. She will be ecstatic, and just plain delighted!"

"I know," laughed The Great Collie. "She will do a fine job, and she won't have time to fret about "them Poodles" as much. Hildegard has been reassigned elsewhere so she won't be around nearly as often. And that's good for Carolyn as well as the rest of us! But I'm taking up your time, Jetaway. You must deliver your messages! I have enjoyed talking with you."

"Thank you, Sir. I will be off, and on my way whenever you say. Also, am I to understand that O'Casey could be at the Landing Site to snap some pictures of the arrival?" Jetaway asked.

"Yes, he will be. Since the new arrival has already been assigned to the Palace, we do want documentary records of the event. And now, Jetaway," said The Great Collie with a twinkle in his eye. "You say the newcomer was a very pampered canine? I bet you were, too!" His Greatness was in a joking mood.

He was so happy that he, with Wrangler helping, had successfully "fixed" Jetaway's devastations, and it was a good feeling to see him smiling again. The Great Collie certainly intended to see O'Casey about further Press Pigeon releases. He knew O'Casey would handle a talkative Bloodhound named Buddy, once he was made aware of what had happened in Jetaway's case. He was enjoying his "post-trauma" visit with this Springer Spaniel, and he found that Jetaway was intelligent as well as responsible. He liked this new friend, and both he and Wrangler intended to see Jetaway often in the future. Under different circumstances, of course! But now, The Great Collie waited for him to respond to an amusing query. At least, His Greatness thought so!

"Well, yes, Sir, I was pampered. It wasn't like this guy, though. Well, it may have been just like that, too! Our humans were pretty intense!" said Jetaway smiling as he remembered.

"I knew it!" laughed The Great Collie. "Your ego is in check, but not so for the newcomer! Right?"

"Right, Sir! He likes himself quite a lot, and his ego runs rampant. Or so Buster says. You know, much like Carolyn's high opinion of herself," smiled Jetaway still waiting to be excused!

"I find that hard to believe!" said The Great Collie laughing again. Carolyn's giant-sized ego was a well known fact in Canine Heaven. Carolyn herself made sure of that!

"Well, we shall see tomorrow when I personally greet this newcomer. I look forward to meeting my Office Boy." His Greatness chuckled. "You must be off,

Jetaway! Oh, I forgot to excuse you. A thousand pardons! You are now excused, my boy. Goodness, what a day! Its been quite a week, too, and I've got a real big idea left to firm up. But, I won't know for sure until a little later. It is a fantastic notion! Wrangler should be back by now! Where is he? I need to go over my idea with him, and I ...yes, Jetaway? Was there something else?"

"I only wanted to say good-bye, Your Greatness," said Jetaway extending his paw.

"I'm sorry," said The Great Collie. "I've had such a busy week, you see. I seem to get absentminded about now. I guess it goes with the territory. Good bye, Jet! I will see you tomorrow. It is off and out for you!" His Greatness chuckled again as he shook the offered paw. "That's one fine Spaniel! A very, very fine Spaniel!" He said to himself when Jetaway took his leave.

Jetaway hurried down the shiny hall on his way out of the Palace. Meeting Wrangler, he gave him a "thumbs-up" as he rushed by. Wrangler smiled, and returned the salute.

"See you tomorrow, Jet. Good luck!"

Jetaway thanked Wrangler, and without further delay, was off to the Senior Community!

THE FAMILY

As Jetaway hurried along on his way to the Senior Community, he was thinking about his Canine Heaven family. He decided to advise the Senior Member of the family first that a new Connection was arriving. The Old Black Dog would expect this consideration! After all, he WAS the Family Patriarch. Yes, The Old Black Dog would know just what had to be done to welcome a newcomer. Jetaway smiled and guessed that's what it meant to be a patriarch! He hurried on faster now!

So Jetaway made his plans. First to where The Old Black Dog resided. Then, he would seek out Rover, and hope that Buster was around, too. Jetaway didn't know what to do about Pasha, the puppy under Lolita's control, but he thought he should advise Lolita anyway, and it might work out. If not, then, he would just have The Old Black Dog handle Lolita! And he would, too! The Old Black Dog didn't like Lolita's bossy ways!

He had been in Canine Heaven longer than any of the other Connections, The Old Black Dog had. He resided with the rest of the Senior Canines in the community designed just for them. The Old Black Dog enjoyed his afterlife in the restful community. He had been a loyal worker on his Master's farm for a long and happy life.

He had earned all the pleasures that he found in Canine Heaven. He was one of the Precious Jewels in the Senior Community which Wrangler mentioned in the Yearly Report. A very real family patriarch, too! His Canine Heaven Connections were very dear with Rover being particularly special.

The two of them, The Old Black Dog and Rover had been together during the old dog's middle years. Rover was only a puppy brought for the human children as a plaything. The older canine never resented the extra attention Rover received as he knew his position was assured in the human family, and Rover's presence was no threat! Rover depended on his leadership, too! With Rover along for company, The Old Black Dog, a happy fellow anyway, was even more so. He watched Rover grow into a black and white shaggy mixed breed of some kind, but it didn't matter. The old dog maybe was mixed himself. In truth, Rover was a mongrel! And he was beautiful! A fluffy tail curled high on his back. A puff on each ear would make any poodle envious! The Old Black Dog loved Rover with a fatherly concern, and Rover returned the love many times over! They were always together, those two.

This happy friendship, coupled with both work and play, went on for a good many years until they became displaced when their human family was broken. It was a related, but very different, environment where they worked the fields and tended the cattle as they were expected to do. Their hearts were not in their work, though. The old days were gone, and they didn't know where! They missed the farm, and they missed their human family. They were grieving, but they still tried their best to serve a strange Master. They gave thanks that they still had each other, and the one bright spot at the end of each day was to snuggle close and dream in the warm touch of the other. This small joy did not last either!

In the third year of their sadness, The Old Black Dog went from the Earth, and Rover was left to serve the household that he loved even less now. With the last link to the old days gone, it was probably the loneliness that caused Rover to enter Canine Heaven before he had reached his ninth year on Earth.

When Rover learned that his friend, The Old Black Dog, was also in Canine Heaven, he was overjoyed, and visited the Senior Community often. Once again they were together, and once again joy filled every moment!

Rover resided on Cloud number four, the Intermediate Community, and having worked outdoors for all of his time on Earth, he was assigned outside duties. Rover tended the beautiful garden that surrounded The Big Bone Palace, and he often invited The Old Black Dog to see his handiwork. Rover was contented! He could be heard singing his "trademark" song, "I'm An Old Country Boy", as he set out bulbs and pulled weeds.

Sometimes on his visits to the Senior Community, Rover and The Old Black Dog sang together. The old canine had his own special song which told of his joys on Earth, and of his awareness as he was leaving it. He sang "My Winter Has Come" in a happy voice, and smiled at his visitor as they both remembered together. The Old Black Dog and Rover had each other again! And it was good!

The two of them had been waiting at the Landing Site to greet Jetaway when he arrived in Canine Heaven. They had not known Jetaway, but when it was revealed to them that he was family, big doings got underway! Jetaway received such a fine and loving welcome that he was all but mystified. Who were these two canines who had their paws wrapped so tightly around him? He was relieved only when he met The Great Collie. The Old Black Dog and Rover continued loving, watching over, and making Jetaway welcome. He reckoned they meant well!

Jetaway remained aloof, though. He knew nothing of a steady farm and family life as Rover and the older canine had experienced. So Jetaway formed his own circle of buddies. Frisky and fun-loving like himself, and always losing their wings, too!

Jetaway had joined his human family as a lively puppy, and remained so for all of his time on Earth. As noted, he was frisky in his afterlife, too! His life on Earth was good with only minor things to complain about. He was overly concerned, though, with events that he could not control. A solar eclipse sent him to bed when the sky darkened, and he never expected to see the light again. As The Great Collie himself had observed, Jetaway was a worrywart!

A great joy to his human family, as best of the bunch; pick of the litter, and all the other good phrases the humans could think of! And with both the humans and Jetaway serving each other, Jetaway had earned his place in Canine Heaven.

He understood the doting natures of his humans, so he did not enter Canine Heaven as a badly spoiled "Pooch". He was just independent with not much interest in family. Until today! But, he thought now, just how often his Canine Heaven family had asked him to be family with them. Jetaway felt a tiny bit of guilt as he remembered. He was here now when the family needed him, wasn't he? He had suffered pain this day, and all for family, too! He remembered his past neglect and excuses, though. But, gee whiz, it wasn't all one-sided!

"You must come more often and visit with Rover and me. We'd sure like that a lot." The Old Black Dog had said.

"Well, I sure will, Sir, when I can find the time. You know the job at the Library keeps me pretty busy." Jetaway usually replied.

Actually, he was just being polite! Jetaway simply didn't enjoy hearing so much singing, and he didn't enjoy conversations having to do with farms and farming activities of which he knew so little about. Rover and the Old Black Dog, it seemed to Jetaway, weren't interested in his life spent around military camps that involved much travel, and they couldn't understand how a canine could have been named, as Jetaway was, for a transmission system of some automobile called an Oldsmobile! Their knowledge of motor vehicles was a Ford or a Chevrolet, and they couldn't even imagine any other kind. They were very polite, though, when they mentioned it to Jetaway. But privately, it was said quite differently!

"Strange! Very strange indeed!" The Old Black Dog would say to Rover.

"Boring! Very boring!" Jetaway said of his visits to the Senior Community. "We stay in touch, and that's enough."

Jetaway knew better than either the Old Black Dog or Rover that their view of family closeness was different from his own feelings. He loved his Canine Heaven Connections, but they shouldn't always have to be together to show the love and concern for each other. Rover and the Old Black Dog were born in the South, and had never traveled for more than a few miles from their home. They were true Southerners where family was family. A great tradition, too! And it was this smothering in that tradition! So, Jetaway made excuses, and today he felt bad about them! But, should he? A little ache told him that he should!

Still, they had kept in touch. Jetaway had accompanied the Old Black Dog and Rover to welcome Pasha, the puppy, when he arrived in Canine Heaven. And later on, Jetaway was with them at the Landing Site to greet Buster. They had been united as a family. Well, almost. Little Pasha had not been along as the family welcomed Buster. Jetaway remembered why, but he was pretty sure that ALL of the family would greet the newcomer together tomorrow.

Pasha, a Cocker-Terrier mix, had no memory of any substance of ever having been on Earth. At times, though, there was a vague feeling that he might have known some doting humans somewhere! He was so happy in Canine Heaven that the thoughts bothered him not at all. His Family Connections bothered Pasha even less! He seldom saw any of them except the Old Black Dog.

The Old Patriarch visited each week at the Puppy Compound. Pasha was ready for a romp anytime, and looked forward to the visits. He loved the old canine and called him grandpa! Rover, Jetaway and Buster only saw Pasha at Chapel or special events. But they loved him, or so they would say to the Old Black Dog when he scolded them for not visiting. They would mention their jobs and just how busy they were with singing in the choir, and other activities, too! They sure intended to spend a lot more time at the Puppy Compound, though! Lolita, the Director of the Compound, was just impossible to deal with anyway. Lolita did not make their efforts pleasant. A lot of excuses the younger canines did make, but they did have a point!

Yes, Lolita could be impossible. It was the beautiful Afghan who had riled the Old Black Dog when Buster had come to Canine Heaven. She had not allowed Pasha to go along with the family when they greeted Buster. The Old Black Dog had spoken his mind, too! Lolita paid little attention to his concerns, for, after all, Pasha was only a puppy with no memory of his time on Earth, so why upset him by greeting a canine that he did not know!

Lolita did promise to be "better informed" if there should be a "next time", though. The Old Black Dog had not argued. There hadn't been time that day. But, he would remember! Yes, Lolita was impossible with very little sense of family! The Old Canine would not suffer her arrogance again! And it was a "next time". Jetaway, hurrying a bit faster to deliver his message, did not worry too much. Pasha WOULD go and welcome the newcomer with the family!

Buster was already a full-grown canine when he came to the human family. He did not serve the family of the Old Black Dog, Rover, Jetaway and Pasha. A loving service to his first Master had earned Buster his place in Canine Heaven. His devotion to his Master was so great that even in his new home, where he was also dearly loved, Buster fixed his eyes in the direction of his first home. Always looking to the Northeast, he waited for his Master to come. And, of course, it could not happen, but he waited just the same. Buster hoped and waited for seven years! He was not unhappy, though. He simply didn't understand his displacement. He remembered his Master's absence, and then one day a moving van came, and then a kind man took him away. Buster had often wished that he had paid more attention at the time. But, he hadn't. So he waited and wondered.

Buster allowed his new human family to love him. He was a beautiful Golden Retriever, so the gentle nature of his breed caused him to respond to the efforts of love in his behalf. He found, though, that he could actually be contented in his new home, and he gave as much of himself as he was able. Every one of the humans seemed to understand Buster's plight, and were happy enough that he was with them. They gave their love freely, and Buster accepted it by becoming an important member of a loving household. But, he did not serve!

Upon arriving in Canine Heaven, and greeted by his only known Connections, Buster kept mainly to himself. He felt no special family ties, but he did see the Old Black Dog from time to time. A very warm welcome was always ready for Buster when he visited the Old Senior. He often worked on the farm with Rover but he seldom encountered Jetaway, and he never did know Pasha. Nevertheless, Buster's afterlife was one of contentment, and he fared much like the other inhabitants of Canine Heaven. He knew his way around even though his shyness kept him from socializing greatly. And he didn't mind a bit, or so he said to himself!

Goodness, who needed a pack of nosy associates bothering a canine who preferred to be alone? Well, Buster did! Who needed a family of Connections one could hardly feel real closeness with? Well, Buster needed that, too! And, it was Freddie who brought out both sides of Buster that he had been denying for so long. The result was perfect!

Freddie was the pretty Curly-Coated Retriever who was organizing a special singing group to perform in the Chapel and elsewhere as well. Freddie decided that a quartet would be more suited to her talents than a trio, or maybe some other form like a quintet. The Chapel, naturally, already had a large chorus, and Freddie often helped with it, so a quartet would be a fine addition. Some personal contribution! Something showcasing her musical abilities, too, and Freddie was plenty smug about that! In no time at all, she was listening very carefully to those who were trying out for the quartet's unique voices.

It was already certain that Freddie herself would sing soprano, and Fresca was chosen for alto. Fresca was a Husky mix with a low throaty twang. Freddie was pleased, and she was very happy with Rusty who was singing the bass voice. Rusty, a Golden Retriever, sang bass in the Chapel Choir as well. Such good luck in finding Fresca and Rusty, and now Freddie needed a tenor, but no satisfactory canine had been found for that important position. She continued to search, and just by chance one day, Freddie heard Buster singing softly to himself as he worked in Fleecy Park. A lot of persuasion took place before he finally agreed to even try out for the tenor voice in Freddie's quartet. Buster was accepted. But still he balked!

"I'm not so sure I can be that much help to you, Ma'am," Buster had said to Freddie. "I'm not a performer, and out front of all those canines, too! Well, I just don't know."

"Nonsense!" She told him. "You are the best! Don't be shy ... develop your talent. And don't fret about those who may be watching you. They're listening to your singing, too! You are doing us all a favor. Now don't be selfish!"

Freddie finally convinced Buster to join the quartet. It was good for him, and, it was good for the quartet. Buster was an excellent choice for he became Freddie's musical partner and was responsible for much of the early success of the quartet. And, as the quartet's popularity grew, Buster was more outgoing in his relations with Canine Heaven residents. He was happy that he was contributing, and his Connections? Well, they were so proud of him! They told him so, too! Buster would forever hold back a bit of himself, though. He didn't know why. He just would!

Jetaway's thoughts were only of the family as he continued on his way, and he decided they were a pretty good lot of Connections, too! He also vowed to be a little closer to all of them. It was nice to have a family, and by this time tomorrow, the family would have a new member. Please, Canis Major, help!

Jetaway delivered his news quickly. The Old Black Dog understood the haste and immediately began to make arrangements for the welcome. He knew what to do. He was the Patriarch. WAS HE NOT?

Jetaway caught up with Rover in the park where he was preparing to take to the lake for a big splash. It was Saturday, wasn't it? Time for the weekly bath. Alright? Without engaging in any banter with Rover, Jetaway advised him of the situation. Rover hurried in his grooming, and went to see how he could help The Old Black Dog. Rover would be at the Senior Community the long night as well. Family business, you know!

Jetaway found Buster at the Chapel. The quartet was busy with their music, but Buster excused himself when he saw Jetaway. The two talked quietly for a moment, and Buster promised to be with the family to greet the newcomer. Buster had known this canine on Earth. He hadn't especially liked him either but he would be there!

The last stop on Jetaway's list was the Puppy Community. After explaining the circumstances to Lolita, he waited for her reply.

"Well, I don't know about this. You came at prayer time, and it is late. I will think about it," Lolita said. "Do make an appointment, and see me in the morning."

In the morning would not be time enough! Jetaway did not argue with Lolita, but he remembered the ugly words between her and The Old Black Dog when Buster had come to Canine Heaven. Little Pasha could not go to greet him! A tired and unhappy Jetaway hurried once again to the Senior Community. The Old Black Dog, his dander up, assured Jetaway that Pasha would be with the family when they greeted the new arrival! Don't worry!

So it was the next morning that the welcoming group was in place. They saw the Big White Eagle deftly land, close his great wings, and quite slowly make his way toward them. They were united as they waited. All five of them! With Pasha included!

At first, Buster stood a little way back from the others. He still seemed to feel that since he was a full-grown canine when he joined the human family, he was not really a bonafide member of the connected family as the others. Of course, The Old Black Dog noticed, and he would have none of it! He drew Buster close, and decreed that Buster and himself stand behind Rover and Jetaway with little Pasha in front of them. It was a balanced and fine looking bunch! The Old Patriarch thought they must be pretty cohesive looking, too! How nice it was to have ALL his family together on this special day.

No one was at the Landing Strip but O'Casey with his camera. O'Casey was a bit surprised to see Pasha standing so obediently in place. He did snap a few close shots of the group, but kept his distance otherwise. O'Casey was there by directive, and he did not intend to disturb their smiling stance. O'Casey did wonder how they managed to get Lolita to allow Pasha out of her sight!

And, of course, it was Lolita's extra effort, as she called her exchange with The Old Black Dog that gave Pasha permission to attend the welcome. But, it was The Old Black Dog who prevailed in the dialogue, and it did not matter how Lolita described it! He had simply told her not to be this doggoned bossy and stubborn when events such as a newcomer's arrival came up. He was noting Lolita's continuing reluctance ... so he played his ACE! He hadn't wanted to!

The Old Black Dog had used his time to come to the Puppy Community, and he would not be defeated again by Lolita. This was unfair! So he finally stated in a determined voice:

"As Patriarch of this family, I can take this matter to Wrangler whose job will be to take it to you know WHO!"

Lolita wasn't worried, but she shot back that she was in full and complete charge of the Puppy Community, and she had been cited by The Great Collie for a most outstanding commitment. So many times and instances she, Lolita, would be applauded! And, she was quite well, very well in fact, respected in Canine Heaven, thank you! Sir, she was after all, the Director here .... and fully in charge! Lolita was a bit angry!

Nevertheless, Pasha was allowed to go along in the company of the Old Dog with the stipulation that Pasha be returned at once to the Puppy Community, and just as soon as His Greatness welcomed the newcomer! The Old Black Dog had replied rather tersely:

"Yes, yes, Miss Director!" And then he told Lolita to go take a dip in the pond at Fleecy Park to cool off!

Not to be outdone and determined to have the last word, Lolita had said:

"Sarcasm is unwelcome where my-puppies might hear it! We are doing you a favor, Sir! Shame!"

O'Casey, of course, had not heard a word of this exchange, but he smiled a smug grin knowing how Lolita could be, and probably was!

"Oh, what a good shot this is going to be!" O'Casey said out loud turning his camera toward the Big White Eagle. Still making a slow approach the Eagle paused as if to collect himself before the final stop where the family waited expectantly for his precious passenger who would make their family complete!

The Big White Eagle came to a halt, ruffled his feathers to alert the passenger that it was time to depart. But the passenger, who had never been hurried or bossed around by anyone seemed to be in no rush! He was Bojangles! A crossbreed of Dalmatian and Springer spaniel ... black and white and handsome as could be! He knew it, too!

As Bojangles looked over his family of Connections, he recognized none but Buster. Buster had resented Bojangles and his spoiled ways, and had even engaged him in a mauling or two. Perhaps he and Buster could be better friends. As Bojangles looked at the family more closely, he saw something wonderful! A fine lot! He forgave Buster right away for misdeeds! He would meet them very soon, but he needed more rest first.

The Big White Eagle was impatiently flapping his wings and still Bojangles made no move to leave the soft feathery seat. It had been a long flight and he told himself he was tired, and should not just be ejected like some missile. That was just what the Big White Eagle was about to do, though! One last wild shake, and Bojangles decided to let go and give Canine Heaven a try! He stepped down.

At once, many paws reached for him, embracing and loving so tenderly. Hey, these guys were indulgent and probably catering, too! Bojangles loved it all. And with their collective paws holding and caressing him, the welcoming group began the walk to The Big Bone Palace.

And O'Casey snapped and focused!

THE CANINE WEEKLY
SPECIAL EDITION

O'Casey was tired as he walked back to the Canine Weekly newsroom. He had worked late the night before, and when it seemed he was ready for rest, something else came up!

First, he had, by himself, prepared the special announcements requested by The Great Collie. Then he needed more space for his own editorial, and would have to add an extra page. It was important to O'Casey that his extra long editorial be in this week's edition. A masterpiece he had written, and as editor, well, he had plenty to say about space! He made the additional space!

The paper was already a day late as decreed by The Great Collie. The residents of Canine Heaven hadn't taken it too kindly since they did look forward to their newspaper each week. O'Casey knew they would understand why it happened when His Greatness delivered his speech this afternoon in Fleecy Park.

It was time for some very important changes to be made in both service and structural personnel. The Great Collie had chosen to inform all the residents at the same time. That is why O'Casey had been instructed to handle the very private business personally, and to be careful that Buddy and Durkin, the two newsroom helpers, did not know what he was secretly working on! Keeping those

Bloodhounds out of the way was no easy task, but O'Casey had managed it! Now, having finished, he had locked the Canine Weekly editions in his office.

Trying to rest some, O'Casey was aroused by a Whippet messenger from The Big Bone Palace with a special summons for his immediate presence! It was unusual and unexpected and the middle of the night as well! O'Casey accompanied the fast walking Whippet to the Palace gate. There he saw the Chow, Hiro, the Mess Kitchen Director along with King, the Rottweiler Maintenance Engineer. A couple of steps behind O'Casey was the Greyhound, Racer, who was the manager of Fleecy Park. Wrangler appeared with his clipboard in paw, and ushered four yawning canines into the office of The Great Collie.

"I apologize, my friends, for disturbing your rest, and I know that you are already tired. O'Casey must be especially weary, but it was a necessity to call this meeting tonight as I have made some special plans for tomorrow." The Great Collie began. "Now I am also aware that O'Casey will meet the White Eagle tomorrow to snap some shots of a special arrival, and he may yet get to sleep if he enlists the help of Durkin and Buddy for this particular chore.

"I am planning an assembly tomorrow afternoon in Fleecy Park of all Canine Heaven residents. I will address them while we all go over a special edition of the Canine Weekly together. In that manner, and through that medium we are revealing the changes we are making as well as other Palace news. O'Casey, we expect that these special editions are ready?"

"Yes, Sir!" O'Casey replied.

"Very well. We shall move on. So we are going to have this assembly and we are going to have a picnic, too! I am sorry that I could not arrive at a decision sooner, but, gentle ones, that's the way things are, and, you will have some nocturnal duty, which I will outline for you now as time is short.

"Hiro, a picnic as I mentioned! You will direct your staff to prepare food enjoyed by us canines at picnics. Some of those delicious frosted scones, and filled tarts, well, you know what must be done. And, Hiro, don't forget those chocolate biscuits with plenty of ice cream ... yum, yum and yummy! Now, Hiro, you have lots to do. You are excused."

Hiro mumbled something about spiced Chinese Noodles as he took his leave.

"Chinese Noodles are good, too! Fix them if you have time!" The Great Collie called after him.

"King, you and Racer are to get the Public Address System in place, and in general, prepare Fleecy Park for these festivities of which I speak. You will need long picnic tables, many drinking bowls, etc. There also must be seating around the stage area to accommodate a varied population. Well, you have done this before but not on such a hurry-up notice. I apologize again while you do extra work tonight. You are excused."

His Greatness was smiling as he excused King and Racer. He knew he could count on them! Now turning to O'Casey, The Great Collie quickly explained the need for the printed flyers to be distributed to each Community director.

"He will see that his residents are properly noti-fied." He went on to say, "You have done these before so you already know the amount to print. Wrangler will pro-vide you with the text. It is a short message. Also, as I said a short time ago, it will be to your advantage to rouse Buddy and Durkin, and here I am telling you how to do a fast printing job! Please forgive me!"

"Yes, Sir, I will use the skills of both Bloodhounds to get the flyers out on time. They will not see the Canine Weekly, Your Greatness. They have been excused since noon, and the copies are locked securely in my office. Getting those guys out of bed this time of the night won't be easy." O'Casey said. "I will see that the job is done per your directions, Your Honor."

"Thank you, O'Casey. Excused!"

Now, it was time for The Great Collie to yawn, and O'Casey heard him say to Wrangler, "Lets get to bed!"

O'Casey had hurried to get the flyers printed with the help of Buddy and Durkin. They had been excited to learn about the picnic, but they also knew a stack of Ca-nine Weekly Newspapers were locked in O'Casey's of-fice, and it was plain that they could not see them. It had been the Bloodhounds who had typed and set that beastly Yearly Report and they couldn't even see the rest of the paper until tomorrow! It was very galling to them!

"Wonder what's so doggoned secret." Buddy had said more to himself than to anyone else. But O'Casey heard it!

"None of your bloody business." O'Casey an-swered. "Call the messenger to deliver these papers, and when that is done, you guys can go on back to your quarters. It's past midnight, and I've got to be at the Landing Site at noon. Now get moving!"

"O'Casey, why do you have to shoot the pictures of that newcomer? Durkin or I could do it with you being so all fired busy," Buddy yawned as he helped Durkin bundle the flyers.

"That is not your business either!" O'Casey yelled. "Keep Moving!"

The messenger arrived, and O'Casey said good night to his helpers. It was a hollow farewell, though, for both of them had curled up behind the linotype and were already asleep. He didn't try to awaken them, and had gone into his own office where he fell asleep at his desk.

This morning, all had gone well at the Landing Site, and the new arrival, Bojangles, was on his way to meet with The Great Collie. O'Casey thought this was a fine looking canine, although he could see right away that this canine sure did like attention, and plenty of it! His welcoming Connections were obliging him, too! O'Casey smiled thinking of the special announcement in the Canine Weekly. Office Boy? It figures!

It was almost time to leave for the big event in Fleecy Park. O'Casey had repacked his camera bag with more film and other supplies. He would shoot the festivities. He would be expected to! He was so tired, he just might let the Bloodhounds, Buddy and Durkin, handle the picture taking. He didn't know yet just what he would do, though! His two helpers loved the photography side of the newspaper business, but they could get carried away. Just snap everything in sight! No, he had better do it himself. This was a very important event, and The Great

Collie would want it to be well-documented. O'Casey would see that it was! That was settled! Now, he must spruce himself up a bit, and take off for Fleecy Park.

O'Casey would personally carry the Canine Weekly newspapers to the park. Once there, he would provide each Community Director with enough copies for the residents of his particular area. These would be passed out at the proper time. O'Casey neatly put the stacks in the newspaper cart, but he couldn't leave right away. He was so tired! Only a minute or two. He brushed around his ears again, and sat down!

O'Casey knew that this was a very, very special edition of his newspaper. He already knew of all the Palace announcements since he had printed them himself the night before. They were of importance, but The Great Collie would handle them in his address. The Yearly Report, also in this edition, would be mentioned by his Greatness as well. He gave these matters no further thought. They would not concern him at all. He did think of his editorial in the same edition, and it was important to him!

O'Casey knew that his "piece" would not have a part in the event at Fleecy Park. He didn't expect it. Nothing official! O'Casey had wanted it read along with the regular weekly news when the festivities were over. That's the way it usually was, and he wanted them to read what he had written this week. Especially this week!

As he rested, O'Casey opened a copy of the Canine Weekly to the Editorial Page. There it was! He read it again:

Canine Heaven

My Brothers and Sisters, perhaps you have noticed the spring in my step, the twinkle in my eye, the joy in my talk. Well, it's all because of Little Ben.

I had a young half-brother on Earth of whom I grew very fond. We were the happiest of playmates one summer when I was full-grown, and he was a puppy, but the joy in our frolic meant a lot to the both of us. He is Little Ben, a lot like me in looks, although his mother was a beautiful Dalmatian. I knew her, too.

Little Ben resides with the puppies right here in Canine Heaven, and I was so happy to find him! Now, as brothers we can spend our afterlife together. I know, of course, that he does not remember me since he was only a puppy at the time, but all this is changing. He will know me again thanks to the Great Collie, and with the help from Lolita, the Puppy Community Director. It seems that Little Ben and I may be the only blood-related inhabitants here. There may be more, but it remains unknown at this time. I ask you to be joyful with me today as you know about Little Ben. A few of you knew already, and I thank each one of you who helped bring us to this day as brothers should be. Canine Heaven is even more dear!

I give thanks to Madeline, the able helper at the Puppy Compound. Her keen sense of justice and family was indeed helpful in removing the obstacles that blocked my relationship with my little brother. I want to thank Wrangler who knew just what to do when he received the information. I want to thank again The Great Collie who acted quickly and decisively in my behalf as well as the rights of Little Ben. I want to thank Lolita, too!

Lolita, as we all know, is the very capable and caring Community Director. She loves all those little fellows as if they were her own. That makes for a happy atmosphere where each puppy will spend a delightful afterlife. And this is good! Perhaps a bit strange to some since she never experienced motherhood on Earth. A terrible attack by a crazy burglar seeking drugs in her Master's home deprived Lolita of ever becoming a mother. She and her sister were very young as they valiantly tried to protect their Master. They could not, and were found badly wounded beside their Master's lifeless body.

Sometimes we think we know the most important things to know about our own Canine Heaven brothers and sisters. We do not, though! Our personal files are sealed, and opened only at our own individual request. This is proper. Lolita gave her permission to share this one item in her file with us. It will explain away any criticism of a beautiful Afghan, who perhaps does her job too well! Lolita's concern for Little Ben's welfare was at the heart of her objection to anything she had not been yet exposed in Canine Heaven such as a real family situation. Happily, for us all, the matter is resolved!

The Great Collie's problem solving expertise also served me well in other matters this past week. I won't share the particulars as they are very, very personal. Thank you, Your Greatness!

I do want to touch on one important thought having to do with matters that have no relevance in Canine Heaven. We all lived on Earth. We served. Otherwise we would not be here enjoying the wonders and love of Canine Heaven. To get here in the first place, we did do something right, and knowing this, our memories will sustain us. We earned an afterlife with our presence here. What caused us grief or pain on Earth must be laid aside. Earth is far, far away. Let it rest! We need it no longer!

I have enjoyed writing this special editorial. I know how different it is from the usual, but they will be back! When you have an opinionated, arrogant and political Irish Wolf Hound like my self ... well, we don't change much. We just pause when appropriate to reflect about good and wonderful things. Good and wonderful things like Little Ben. Good and wonderful things such as the wisdom and vision of The Great Collie. All the good and wonderful things that make friendship what it is for us all!

I bid you peace and joy!

O'Casey was pleased as he finished reading. He had been pleased each time he had read it, and he had been pleased when he had finished writing his editorial, too! It was so unlike what he had wanted to say at first which was a vicious attack on Lolita and her dominant attitude at the Puppy Compound. A battered and frustrated O'Casey needed an outlet! But, he reconsidered!

After hearing Lolita's story about the brutal attack on her in her puppyhood, O'Casey had personally talked to her. He obtained her permission to let it be told. She wasn't a bad sort when one got to know her. Lolita would forever be Lolita, though, and that would be alright, too, when there was understanding!

O'Casey rose, checked the newspaper cart again, and after brushing his hair and putting on a gold studded collar, took off for Fleecy Park.

THE PROGRAM
AT FLEECY PARK

When O'Casey arrived at the Park, he was relieved immediately of his burden by a helper from The Big Bone Palace. The helper, actually a lesser aide to The Great Collie, and an active Whippet, too, would distribute the copies of the Canine Weekly to the Community Directors. O'Casey's job was now over, and he could enjoy the festivities. He sat down to rest, and another bustling Whippet brought him a bowl of flavored water, smiled warmly, and hurried off.

As O'Casey sipped the cool refreshment, he noticed the long picnic tables ready for Hiro's caterers, and he also noticed that most of the residents had already gathered in the Park. And they were clearly enjoying themselves, too! The Seniors had just arrived but Lolita had not yet brought in the puppies. So far, though, everyone seemed happy and excited. They loved events like this! Spirits were high! O'Casey rested and watched with little energy, and not a whole lot of interest either. Just too doggoned tired!

The Old Black Dog, along with Rover and Jetaway came directly to the Park after The Great Collie had personally greeted Bojangles. Buster was singing with the quartet so he had gone to the Chapel to join Freddie and the others, and Pasha had been returned in keeping with

Lolita's instructions. Bojangles was looking over the village. He would only be a minute, he said. He was sure having a fine time on his first day in Canine Heaven!

A small black shaggy dog named Noodles stopped by to talk with Bojangles. Noodles had known him on Earth, and it was good to see Bojangles, he said! He was quite a nice canine, Noodles was, and the Old Black Dog asked him to eat with Bojangles' family at the picnic.

Carolyn and Lucy were chatting and laughing as usual. Having no official duties this day, they were simply enjoying themselves, although Carolyn's insides were all "atwitter" as she was wondering if The Great Collie would actually make his choice known today for the Most Private Secretary position.

Carolyn tried to relax, and she did a good job of being outwardly charming and joyful. She just couldn't think of any canine more qualified! His Greatness couldn't prefer another Whippet, or, heaven forbid, a Poodle? No, if he decides today, or any day, then it only can be Carolyn, she reasoned. But, what if...? No, Carolyn is the best!

Racer, being the Director of Fleecy Park, busied himself seeing that there were fun things to do for every breed and size of Canine Heaven inhabitants. He was proud that he had been able to accomplish so much in the short while since late last night when he had just learned of the festivities. And everything had come together real well with the picnic tables, planned activities, and he had helped King set up the Public Address System and ready the Park, too. Proud, yes, but like the others on duty since the night before, Racer was tired. It was all worth it though, and he was sure Hiro, King and O'Casey all felt the same way!

Racer paused long enough to enjoy a refreshing drink with O'Casey, and together they rested for awhile. It was nice! O'Casey's obligation for the affair was over, but Racer knew that he, himself, could not lay his own head to rest until the last canine had departed Fleecy Park. All the smiling faces and everyone wearing their Sunday best collars ... well, it was energizing ... so Racer kept racing around!

Just about everyone did wear dress-up collars, and some even had cufflets and anklets on, too. Hildegard perhaps was the most fancy which surprised no one. She wore a beautiful jeweled collar and both cufflets and anklets. All perfectly matched, of course! Carolyn, who had chosen a soft leather ornament of pastel colors, stopped to chat with Hildegard.

"Why, Hildegard," she quipped, "how stunning you do look! My goodness, you have more jewels on than a queen."

"Thank you, my dear," Hildegard replied. "Here are the treasures I wore to an event in Paris. We heard a great cello player that day."

"How nice," Carolyn went on. "Just about everybody likes jello."

"Yes, dear," Hildegard mumbled, not bothering to explain. She had already decided that this Carolyn creature was needling her.

Hildegard moved on and assuming the role of unofficial hostess, she sought out Racer to offer her services. Racer was much too busy for this kind of interference. He thanked Hildegard, and explained that everything was already taken care of and under control. Racer was trying to be polite, but Hildegard was not satisfied. Surely a hostess was needed for such an important event as this, and who could be better prepared than herself? Experience in so many of the fine dramas in the wonderful world of Royalty, and the grandeur of drawing rooms in New York, Paris and London and other great cities, too. Hildegard was clearly a nuisance, but he did not want to be impolite to a Senior. King happened to come along seeking Racer's help in the viewing area seating. This was important and urgent, and noticing also that Racer was trapped by Hildegard, King took charge. He simply told Hildegard that she should please go on and let Racer and himself work!

"Well, I do declare!" Hildegard retorted sharply. "Such uncouth response to an offer of help!"

"Yes, Ma'am," King said, as he hurried off with Racer.

Undaunted, a little wounded though, Hildegard moved toward the giant stage hastily erected for today's festivities. There she saw Freddie going over the quartet numbers with Rusty, Fresca and Buster.

"My dear," Hildegard said to Freddie. "I believe you would be more elegant if you tilted your head slightly to the left when you sing. I heard and saw a marvelous quartet once in Bombay where the voice was made softer by assuming this position. Have you tried it?"

"No, ma'am," said Freddie. "We will try it sometime, but not today. Thank you for your concern."

Freddie went on with her work. She smiled at Hildegard, though. Must be a bit nice to the Seniors, no matter how big a nuisance they are. Just be nice!

Hildegard saw that Lolita, with the puppies in tow had arrived. No need to offer any advice there! Hildegard did find comfort, though, when she came up on a dozing O'Casey. He was too tired to walk away and too tired to visit. A few yes, ma'ams and no, ma'ams was the best he could do while Hildegard spoke of the great newspapers and magazines she had known in her earlier days. Of course, these were the Paris, New York and London publications. Marvelous, my dear! Simply marvelous! Hildegard made no effort to move on. She was clearly enjoying herself, and she had the kind of audience she loved ... captive.

O'Casey was relieved when a Whippet aide brought him the message that Holy Joe and he would occupy stage seating during the program as well as the rest of the stage activities which included The Great Collie's address. This was a surprise, and O'Casey would not be expected to handle the photography after all. This meant he had to call on Buddy and Durkin and organize them. There wasn't much time, so he hastily extricated himself from the mental clutches of Hildegard, and summoned the Bloodhounds. They were delighted. Now they could finally show O'Casey what a fine photographic team they could be. Very professional and all! Since he had no other choice, O'Casey smiled at their enthusiasm, and went back to dozing!

Lolita was met at the Park entrance by efficient Whippet aides who escorted her and her charges to the special seats set aside for them. Lolita was a mite unhappy when she noticed the Toys were to be seated directly behind the puppies in the viewing area.

"This will not do," Lolita said.

However, before she could voice her objection, Baby Collette began to cry.

"Yoyita, Yoyita!" she wailed, "This Pomrani pushed me, and he pu-pu-pulled my yittle pretty ears."

Hurrying to calm the puppy, Lolita told the offending Pomeranian to be on his best behavior, and refrain from an action that would cause her to come to the necessary action of notifying Constable Napoleon! The Pomeranian didn't take too kindly to Lolita's arrogance, and as she tended another puppy, whispered to Baby Collette that she was an awful crybaby, and a smarty pants!

"Yoyita, Yoyita," she wailed again. "Now he "cally" me bad names!"

Summoning the Supervisor of the Toy Community, Lolita demanded that he reseat his charges in another section of the viewing area near the stage.

"Well, I don't know, Ma'am," Poncho, a Mexican Chihuahua, told her. "These seats were assigned to us, and most of us are here already. The program is to begin shortly. Maybe you could somehow quiet the puppies down! That Baby Collette in particular."

Lolita, without bothering to argue, directed a Whippet aide to bring Racer immediately to the viewing area. After admonishing Racer soundly for an inexcusable lapse in acceptable judgement by seating those "dwarf" canines close to the puppies! The two sizes could in no way be compatible, and this must be corrected at once! Racer saw no problem, but he relocated the Toys anyway. Lolita thanked Racer, and said nothing to Poncho!

Poncho could not take kindly to Lolita's treatment of his breed. Dwarfs, indeed! He knew it was a rule to defer to the Seniors and the puppies. He did not mind that at all. He did mind Lolita's attitude and arrogance. And, he told Racer so!

"Well, thank you for being so nice, Poncho," Racer told him. "We all know Lolita, and this was no time to get in an argument with her. You have better seating anyway, but I understand where you're coming from, and you are right, of course, to feel as you do. You did make things easier for me by not raising a fuss about all this. I do think the seating is better for you, though. So thank you again!"

"Yeah, you're right, Racer. It is a lot better here. We do not need frisky little monsters bothering us! They do no wrong according to Lolita, but you know?" Poncho laughed. "That Baby Collette is just a miniature Hildegard!"

Racer laughed with Poncho. It was a fact! Baby Collette was, in many ways, just like Hildegard. Racer slapped his thighs, and was still chuckling when he told King. They laughed together. Both needed a good laugh on this day, or so they said. Like O'Casey, they were all tired out. Can't drop just yet!

Racer and King, the perfectionists, made their final assessment of the arc around the stage, and the stage itself as well. It looked good! A first class job, and they were pleased!

The seats on the stage were for the Canine Council and The Great Collie. A trio of seats placed to the right were for O'Casey, Holy Joe and Wrangler. Of course, His Greatness needed his three most important residents near for consultation or advice! Gertrude was softly playing the organ mounted on a low platform by the stage. Wrangler, clipboard in paw, stepped to the podium:

"Brothers and Sisters," he began in a happy voice. "Welcome to our special coming together. His Greatness will be so pleased to see all of you! Now, let me introduce our distinguished Council of Canines. All fine Whippets. Like me in every way! A little joke there!"

A wild clapping of paws, and an ear splitting yapping as well. This crowd wasn't all that interested in the Canine Council members, but they did enjoy Wrangler's jokes!

"Thank you. First, in Position One, we have Leopold; Position Two is Bonaparte; Position Three is Nathanial and Position four is Caesar. Please take a seat, Gentle Canines. Thank you! (some clapping,) Rounding out the other notables with us today, will be Holy Joe, our Chaplain, (A vigorous and expected clapping) and O'Casey, the editor of our fine Canine Weekly!"

Subdued clapping. O'Casey was simply not as popular as Holy Joe!

"Now," Wrangler went on. "Entering Fleecy Park, and gracing our stage, is His Greatness, The Great Collie!"

A wild enthusiastic welcome for the head of all
Canine Heaven! It was always hard to tell whether the
populace loved or respected him more. They were mighty
pleased with His Greatness. He would forever hold them
in his care. A "given" was what he meant to them, so the
residents gave a respectful ear as The Great Collie spoke.

"My dear Comrades of Canine Heaven, I welcome
you. This is a wonderful day for us all; a coming together
to share ideas, and to learn from each other. I shall address you very shortly. First, though, let's enjoy the program."

"Thank you, Your Greatness," Wrangler said.
"Before we proceed, however, Holy Joe will give our
happy event his ever-warming blessing."

"Thank you, Wrangler," Holy Joe began. "We
ask only of Canis Major, that his love shine on us this
day. May we all find something to our liking as we go
forth into the fellowship and goodwill that this event is
all about!"

"Thank you, Holy Joe," Wrangler was smiling at
the joy of the crowd. Overwhelming! And he was pleased
about all of it. The crowd, the enthusiasm, the whole
thing! Not much time to bring it together. But they had!
Everyone working together was the answer. Wrangler
was still smiling as he stepped aside, and the program
began.

First, a couple of the puppies said little poems,
and a fluffy Poodle did some ring jumping. Then, several Dachshunds acted out a comedy skit called "The Long
and Short of It". The crowd really enjoyed this, and, at
times, it was difficult to hear above the roar.

Rover sang "I'm Just an Old Country Boy", and Elmo, the Fox Terrier, played the guitar. The crowd joined in the singing when Rover sang the last verse of the song. It was quite moving!

> Folks are happiest on the land
> Where neighbors give a helping hand.
> Where a smile means goodwill,
> And not, I'll send you a "bill".
> A country boy! A country boy!

Many of the canines remembered the ways of old time country neighbors. It was a time that was long gone on Earth as the Modern World evolved. In Canine Heaven, though, progress will be made, but neighborliness would continue forever. How wonderful, they thought, and gave Rover a standing ovation!

Rover bowed several times while always looking toward the Old Black Dog for his approval, and it was there! The Old Black Dog beamed and smiled. Even The Great Collie shook Rover's paw and told him the standing ovation was well earned. The paw shaking was very unexpected, and Rover just knew he was going to faint! But he didn't! He accepted the honor graciously, and returned to his seat still smiling. He knew he had done a good job, and His Greatness had actually touched him, too! Great!

The Great Collie had really enjoyed Rover's song, and like the others, he knew that modern and electronic times had lost neighborliness to a large degree. This made him sad, and while two pretty Pekingese sang a duet, he still thought about Rover's song.

"Why, I can remember when everybody was truly his neighbor's keeper," The Great Collie mused to himself. "In the old days in Montana, everyone cared about everyone else in the village, and that went for the canines, too."

Yes, the canines, too. Especially, for the Collie who wore no particular Master's collar. The Collie, it seemed, just belonged to the village somehow, and no one knew exactly why. He showed up one morning near the livery stable, and was hardly more than a puppy. Maybe the young Collie liked the village, because he stayed and became a partner with the people of the village. Everyone loved the friendly canine, fed and frolicked with him, but no one claimed the Collie. He was welcome everywhere, and the only name he ever acquired was simply "Collie". As he grew, he seemed be all places at once and always ready to serve his adopted village!

Maybe his talents were necessary to chase the cows from old Mrs. Miller's garden, or maybe he watched the little children at play, or on their way home from school. Maybe he was guiding some elderly citizen safely across a dusty or muddy road. Maybe someone was sick, and he bedded down at their place, until the crisis was over. Maybe the ice man needed help, or the mailman needed help to retrieve the mail sacks tossed from a passing train. Maybe the livery stable boy needed help, or the milkman could use him, or the Constable. Maybe even the Minister needed help at times to get the parishioners to church on a sleepy Sunday. "Collie" was always on duty!

The Collie performed such a variety of services and functions that the inhabitants could not imagine life in the village without "Collie". And "Collie" could not imagine it either! He often wondered if he had contributed to the goodwill and neighborliness among the people by his faithfulness and caring. He did not really know how else to behave! But, he was part of the Village, too! Therefore, he HAD contributed!

"Now I'm The Great Collie," he whispered to himself. The two Pekingese', having finished their duet, were taking their bows. "I'm sorry, but I guess I didn't hear much of the song with lots on my mind today, and I get to thinking of that Collie of long ago. Could I have reached this plateau in Canine Heaven without him? No! He served, and he served a whole village. I don't see it as any surprise, considering my advancement, that old country goodness along with neighborliness is still high in my expectations! But, hey, I've got a job to do! Begone, old memories!"

One old memory did not immediately vanish, however. The Great Collie was remembering the day he arrived at the Briefing Center. He was met by the two top Canines, who without saying a word, placed the Great Seal of Canine Heaven around his neck. Somehow, he knew what it meant, but he listened to their instructions anyway. Actually the Center Manager and Chief Supervisor had very few suggestions for His Greatness. And they now addressed him as such, but he himself, had said nothing and asked no questions. The Collie knew. And he was humble in his heart!

"Your Greatness, The Great Collie," The Saluki Manager said. "You will immediately leave for Canine Heaven. The Big Bone Palace is your quarters, and also your place of rule. The last, and perhaps most important item we give to you is The Great Charter. You, and no one else, will have an interpretation. You will use this information wisely. Off with you, your Greatness, and have a most successful and long rule! Ready for your boarding, the Big White Eagle awaits!"

Then The Great Collie was on his way to Canine Heaven. He still had not spoken, and was silent until welcomed by the Canine Council.

"Greetings, your Greatness."

"As you were," he answered.

A long time ago. A very, very long time. Now in his one hundred and twenty-seventh year of rule, His Greatness had to smile. Holy Joe and Wrangler on a mission to solve the mystery of The Great Charter, and maybe one day, they would find the key! And one day, maybe he would help them! Right now, though, he was going to enjoy himself.

The Great Collie, coming out of his reverie just in time to see four Greyhounds do an acrobatic routine. Now it was time for the quartet.

"Toot, Toot," the canines yelled!

They wanted to hear the most popular quartet number, "Toot, Toot, Toot, Toot My Golden Flute". Gertrude played the melody, and Jetaway with his bass flute pointed directly toward Sirius, began to make the flute sound like a horn!

"Toot, Toot," the crowd yelled over and over until the quartet began singing. And the canines joined in the fun! Especially the chorus, which they sang with plenty of gusto!

Toot, Toot, Toot, Toot my golden flute
That I have played and played.
I will bring my message clear
Since I've been away!
To have and hold and point the way-
Then I will know for sure,
That my flute, my golden flute
That I have played before!

Such wild clapping and yapping joy, and Jetaway was at his best! The more he "tooted", the more they wanted, and even The Great Collie tapped his foot, and joined the singing, too!

With all of this exuberant and joyful behavior, the quartet did not even try to do all the songs they had ready for this event. Just "Toot, Toot", until Wrangler intervened reluctantly. A quieting down, however, had to be done for The Great Collie's address, and to have time for the picnic.

"Oh, my!" Wrangler called out. "I'm "Toot Tooted" out, and out of breath!"

"Toot, Toot," the canines called as they were still loudly clapping, their toes tapping, and their voices happily yapping!

"No! No way! No more! No how!" Now, Wrangler was yelling for order. He had to move on. There was so much to do!

"Brothers and Sisters, please quiet yourselves, and please give to me your attention! It is a pleasure to once again introduce His Greatness, your one and only Great Collie!"

Silence! Then, a dignified and subdued clapped welcome.

"Your Greatness," Wrangler said.

The Great Collie was casual in his grooming for this event. No ornate and bejeweled symbols of office graced his collar.

"This is an official meeting, and a picnic, too," he had told his Whippet groomer, Blue, this morning. "And I can certainly conduct official business in a plain leather collar with my seal of office attached. You know the gold one with the gold chain? Yes, that's it! I want to enjoy the picnic without being all weighted down. So just that medallion, alright? And only brush and clip where necessary. No more than that."

"Yes, Your Greatness," Blue agreed. "Your choices are excellent!"

And as The Great Collie stepped before the microphone, he looked just as a regular Collie resident. Almost anyway! One difference, of course, was an elaborate medallion with the Great Seal of Canine Heaven clearly visible. What a difference it made, too!

"Brothers and Sisters, welcome once again! I can see you are having a good time, and I am happy because a few of our most dedicated servants worked almost through the night to prepare this joyful coming together for us. Let us show our appreciation for O'Casey. He made sure you received your invitation on time, and for both King and Racer, who readied Fleecy Park for our enjoyment and convenience. And now, we will show our appreciation for Hiro! Oh, we know who he is. Yum, yum yummy. And we will partake of the wonderful picnic a little later. Yummy!"

Wild and roaring applause!

"But first, we must conduct our important business," His Greatness said. "Business that is of interest to each of you. Please open your Canine Weekly Newspapers to page one, and read along with me as I explain each item. Retain this newspaper, and refer to it if you need to. You must be familiar with the official changes made in Canine Heaven today.

"Also, in this issue of your Canine Weekly, you will see the Yearly Report from my office. Most of you know about it already, but it is published every year for the benefit of new arrivals. We urge them to read it!

"Your newspaper, along with general news, you will also find an uplifting and heartwarming editorial by O'Casey, our fine Editor. You will not want to miss it.

"Now, we are ready to proceed. And I thank you for your continuing attention."

The canines had become so quiet and attentive that it was hard to think it was the same boisterous crowd enjoying the entertainment a short time before. Lolita had directed her helpers to see the puppies to their play space in the Park. Lolita sat with Carolyn and Lucy to hear The Great Collie's address. It seemed all the Connections were seated together, eager and expectant to learn what His Greatness had to tell them!

"Our first item," The Great Collie began, "is that we only have a limited access with Earth in communications ... access that is mostly via the Briefing Center to my office. It is one-way! We cannot respond or contact them. There is little need to comment on the Press Pigeon service to the Canine Weekly. I know it is somewhat helpful, but their service is also limited, and not accurate at times either.

"We do want to correct this non-communication with Earth the best we can. We want Earth to know of our wondrous society in Canine Heaven. We want them to know that the joys of our afterlife was made possible through our services on Earth. Canine Heaven is strictly a service oriented attainment as you already know. We want Earth to know what we know, and this will happen one day.

"We are going to get ready for that time! Therefore, today I am creating a science and research laboratory. The technicians will begin to work on this project right away. We may be successful. We may not! Nevertheless we shall try! Roberto, a Great Dane, will head this endeavor. He is well-qualified. I am told he learned from his Master, an accomplished scientist in the field of electronics. Roberto will have as his first assistant a fine Boxer, Jeffery. Jeffery knows chemistry! Enough said."

A low surprised murmuring was heard among the canines. Communications with Earth? This was big! Those seated near Roberto and Jeffery shook their paw and wished them well!

"Now," The Great Collie continued. "When, not if, we establish contact, I want to have a history of our society already prepared. Therefore, as Chief Historian for this project, I appoint Lucy, our Librarian. Her office will be located beside the Newspaper facility. Her work will begin at once. Would you please stand, Lucy?"

"Lucy," Carolyn whispered, "this is so nice for you! Will I be left all alone in the Library?"

"No, you won't!" Lucy whispered. "I think His Greatness has something else in mind for you."

"Now, don't you tease me," Carolyn said as Lucy smiled gracefully and accepted congratulations. Carolyn didn't want to think that maybe, just maybe, The Great Collie would name his choice for The Most Private Secretary today. Maybe she could dream. Just a little!

The big question on everyone's mind right now was who would be the new Librarian. Carolyn? They knew she adored the Library, but her heart was set on the Secretary position. Who then? They did not have to wait long, however!

"With Lucy reassigned, we needed to fill the position of Librarian. I have appointed Jetaway! Jetaway is our best upward achiever for this challenge. He has prepared himself well. He was one of Lucy's First Assistants along with Carolyn. He will choose his assistants to work with him. Where are you, Jet?" The Great Collie called out.

Jetaway stood, and waved his paw at His Greatness. He blew a kiss to Lucy, too! She had helped him so much in his early days at the Library. Lucy smiled at Jetaway, and quipped, "Better not be losing your wings now. You got work to do! No time to be worrying either!"

The canines laughed and clapped at Lucy's loving council to Jetaway. They knew how easy it was for him to be deprived of his wings, and they knew of his constant fretting, too!. Laughing along with them, Jetaway knew Lucy was right. With this important job, he resolved to do better!

"Alright!" The Great Collie smiled. "We will all help Jetaway stay out of trouble. Let's do another round of applause for him."

After the clapping, Jetaway turned to the Old Black Dog and smiled. Smiling just as broadly, the Senior Canine put his paw around Jetaway, and gently whispered to him, "Well done, my boy! Very well done!"

Getting the attention of the crowd, The Great Collie continued:

"A change of the Chapel Organist is also announced today. Gertrude played the Chapel organ efficiently for quite some time, and has delighted us today with her expertise. Gertrude will devote her talents to the advancement of our population in the musical field. A particular group who will benefit will be the puppies. They can learn how the scales relate to the tunes, and eventually master the less sophisticated of the musical instruments, and ... *yes, my* dear?"

Lolita's paw had shot up requesting recognition!

"Your Greatness, please pardon this intrusion, but as Director of the Puppy Community, and knowing their abilities, as well as their limitations, I request that I be consulted on all aspects of this undertaking." Lolita was speaking quite emotionally! A Whippet aide hurried over to her, and thrust a microphone in her face.

"Your Greatness," Lolita said. "This project will need further study in my opinion. Maybe I am to be replaced as Director, which would be most unfortunate for the puppies. I am only seeking to understand, and if I continue as Director, then I must be consulted. It is absolutely necessary! Thank you!"

Lolita had finished speaking, or so it seemed, as she sat down. Actually, she was waiting to hear how The Great Collie responded to her interruption of his address. Surely, he would agree that it was necessary! Lolita told the Whippet, still holding the microphone, to get lost!

"Dear Lolita," The Great Collie was smiling. "Of course, your advice is of great importance in getting this idea to work, and you will be consulted immediately, too! As Director, you will not be replaced. The puppies would not allow it, and frankly we just wouldn't dare!"

His Greatness was still smiling and he was joking a little, too. He knew a project that had to do with the Puppy Community would bring a challenge from the bossy and arrogant Lolita. He expected it, but he was going to move on anyway with the idea. Lolita would embrace it once she was fully informed. The Great Collie knew this, too!

"Wrangler has the worksheet for the project as well as Gertrude. This does provide for your participation. So, my dear, at ease!"

"Thank you, Your Greatness," Lolita replied, and sat down again.

"Mercy me, Lolita! How you can get all worked up!" Carolyn told her.

"Oh, hush!" Lolita hissed. "You do not understand puppies."

"Yes, I do," Carolyn said. "I was a little puppy once!"

"Big deal!" Lolita said as The Great Collie began to speak.

"Well, this is settled, Now we know that the Director of the Puppy Community will continue to be Lolita. Seems she is stuck with this job again!"

Everyone clapped happily. They knew Lolita would never feel "stuck" taking care of the puppies.

"Now," said His Greatness, taking a deep breath. "I believe we can go forward with the changes in the Music Department. As I said, Gertrude will be devoting her time to musical endeavors other than the Chapel. Freddie will be the new organist for the Chapel in addition to her duties as Quartet Director. And the chorus also will be under Freddie's direction. Hildegard will be assisting at the Chapel in any and all capacities that meet the needs of Holy Joe and Freddie. Ladies, please stand and accept our congratulations!"

They were quite an interesting trio as they smiled and waved. Gertrude was plain, unadorned and matronly. She was all business. No fanfare or any kindly mention was ever fully appreciated. On the other hand, Freddie loved applause, and was in fine form today to receive, and to appreciate, too! She knew very well just how accomplished she was. It was pleasing to know others noticed as well! Freddie was pretty standing beside Gertrude

... girlish, with a silver comb over each ear. And then there was Hildegard!

Hildegard, with her jewels, was already a sight to see, but her hair was puffed in all the right places, too! A stunning Senior French Poodle! She was never out of character either. She assumed the final applause was meant for her since neither Gertrude or Freddie seemed to know the arts of bowing and curtsying! Hildegard did both several times. Perfectly! Oh well, Hildegard was Hildegard, and no society was ever complete without their Hildegards. Canine Heaven's society was no different!

"Thank you, Ladies," The Great Collie said. "I shall continue with a few words about the Yearly Report. Changes in personnel that will be different, we have already handled. All other heads of positions remain the same. What we are basically doing today is adding a set of new programs and facilities. We know you will be happy to hear that it may be possible to add new personnel. A nice task indeed! But no more will be transferred to other positions."

That did it! None of their favorite canines would be replaced or otherwise reassigned. Not Holy Joe, not O'Casey, not King, not Racer, not Claudius, and certainly not Hiro! The crowd clapped happily! Who were these new additions going to be anyway?

"Thank you so much," His Greatness smiled. "I believe you like these guys quite a bit. Particularly Hiro! Yummy, yum, yum? Great! Now to get on ...

"We have needed a grooming salon for some time. Now we will have one! Madeline, an English Sheepdog, and former employee at the Puppy Compound, will be the head of the salon. Madeline was an able worker on a horse ranch on Earth. She knows brushing and shampooing very well! Her chief male assistant will be the talented French Poodle, Sir Echo. He will be grooming the male residents of Canine Heaven, and Madeline will be serving the female population.

"The "Brush and Clip" salon located near the entrance to Fleecy Park, is a new structure, and should be available in a few weeks. You will need appointments, so call the receptionist before you need the service! How about that?"

Yes, this was a great idea. A salon to handle their special grooming needs was a fine, fine idea! The canines did appreciate it so much, and wondered if it might be Hildegard's suggestion. It didn't really matter, though, and they applauded a long time to show approval as Madeline and Sir Echo bowed. Super!

"Thank you," The Great Collie said. "I see you like this project. Well, it was Blue's idea. You know Blue. He was talking to Sir Echo about it, and they talked to Madeline, and someone talked to Wrangler. Wrangler talked to me and after all that talking, the salon is a reality, or will be. Yes, I am talking about the Whippet Blue, who is also my valet. Now with all this talk, and you approving like this, I am glad. Whew!"

More clapping, yeas and alrights!

"The Message Center headed at present by my personal Whippet aides, will remain unchanged. There's one addition to the staff, however. I have directed Noodles, a Terrier-Spaniel, to report to the Chief Whippet at the Center for his assignments, which will consist of Council Business for the most part. It will be a supplement to the operations of the Messenger Fleet only. In no way will Noodles' duties be a part of that service. Noodles will also be a friend of The Big Bone Palace because he will work with my personal office boy. Yes, my OFFICE BOY, Bojangles, who just arrived in Canine Heaven today. We will talk a little about him before we welcome Noodles. Then we can congratulate both Noodles and Bojangles at the same time. As I said, they will be working together a lot.

"Bojangles is a Crossbreed Spaniel and Dalmatian. He was at the Briefing Center for ten years. Now he is here, and is going to be my office boy. For all my years, I have never had an old-fashioned, bona fide office boy. Well, I am going to have one! I am as happy about this as a puppy with a new ball. Bojangles is an excellent choice. Alright now, Noodles and Bojangles, will you both please stand so we can get to know you better!"

Noodles and Bojangles were sitting together anyway, along with Bojangles connected family. When they stood side by side accepting their applause, they made a fine looking pair. And working in, or about the Palace, was quite an honor for both of them.

The Old Black Dog was proud! All in his Heavenly Family had been honored, and so had the little canine, Noodles, who had no known Connections. Well, he had Connections now, the Old Black Dog decreed. Noodles would be part of this family, too! And Noodles was delighted at that happy thought. A family? Right on!

The Old Black Dog told them all how proud he was. Here was Jetaway, as the Librarian, Rover's song, and him shaking paws with His Greatness, and Buster singing in the quartet. Bojangles, as office boy to The Great Collie, and little Noodles doing almost the same job as Bojangles would be. Just in different places! It was a happy bunch that were talking about their good fortunes, and Bojangles decided that this just might work out here in Canine Heaven! He had been here only a few hours, and now he was ... well, he was doing pretty well!

The crowd expected The Great Collie to finish his address soon, as all the items in the Canine Weekly had already been handled. They looked forward now to the picnic, and they wanted to read O'Casey's editorial. The Seniors were a little tired, although they approved the changes and reassignments. They especially approved of the Science and Research Laboratory, and they approved of the idea of the grooming salon. It was the others, too, who wanted to move on to the picnic tables. All that sitting and clapping made them hungry, and if all the business was taken care of, why the delay?

The canines sat rapt, however, when The Great Collie said, that before excusing them, there were a few more important announcements to make. He was sorry, but these items needed more editing, so they could not appear in the Canine Weekly. No one understood this explanation, and didn't need to! Their attention had been rejuvenated, and it was no problem when His Greatness said something was important, it was! They listened intently as Wrangler was once again called to the podium.

"The first announcement is that one fine, trustworthy, hardworking and intelligent Whippet will continue to be my Staff Chief! Take a bow, Wrangler! Everyone knows of your excellent contributions to this society. And, quite frankly, I don't think we could get along without you!"

Wrangler stood beside His Greatness and waved with his one free paw ... that ever present clipboard was clutched in the other! The clapping went on and on amid a thunderous roar. Wrangler was a tremendous asset to Canine Heaven, and next to The Great Collie, Wrangler was the most important and influential canine at The Big Bone Palace. There for them? Always! They clapped some more.

"Very nice! Very nice! and Wrangler deserves your applause a hundred-fold! I say, let's do it again!"

After another earsplitting round of clapping and yelling, The Great Collie thanked them and moved to his last announcement of this official meeting.

"Most Private Secretary position to The Great Collie is second only to the Staff Chief at The Big Bone Palace. It was Gretchen, a capable Whippet, whose tenure is over at the Palace. She will now be assistant to the Historian. We have interviewed many worthy canines, and we have made our decision."

Carolyn's insides were moving every bit as fast as her paws were shaking. She was sitting with Lucy and Lolita, and held tightly to a paw of each one!

"Oh, Canis Major," Carolyn said almost aloud. "Am I not worthy?"

Lucy and Lolita squeezed the trembling paws lovingly as The Great Collie spoke again.

"So without further debate or speculation, I hereby appoint Carolyn to be Most Private Secretary. Carolyn, my dear, would you please join me here at the podium?"

Carolyn, who usually had a quip for every situation was speechless! Lolita and Lucy embraced her, and pushed her toward the stage. Carolyn was truly in a daze!

"Go on, go on!" Lucy urged. "You've been waiting for this. Go!"

"For goodness sakes, Carolyn!" said Lolita. "Move it! We are so happy for you, and this is a big deal!"

Carolyn smiled at her friends. Then Carolyn took charge of Carolyn, and at once moved elegantly toward the stage. And the crowd clapped its joy!

"Welcome, my dear," said The Great Collie. "A very warm welcome to you."

"Thank you, Your Greatness," Carolyn managed to say. "I will do my very best."

Wrangler shook her paw, and at the same time told her to say a few words. A little acceptance speech, you know!! At his urging, Carolyn moved closer to the microphone. She wouldn't say much. Just accept the position. Smile a lot, and make certain every canine knew who Carolyn was! She would be the best! A best speaker, too? Maybe! We'll see!

"Thank you for your welcome. I hope I can meet your expectations as I move into my new position," Carolyn said in a trembling but forceful voice. "There are many good things in Canine Heaven, and a lot of them have happened to me. I am most grateful to two good friends that I respect greatly. They know who they are! Thank you both very much.

"Besides my pretty coat and queenly bearing, I do have a lot to offer this important challenge. I have intellect, and I now have book learning. My verbal usage is much improved, but I could not, and did not, plan that it happen! Sometimes I digress in this area. I do not apologize! My environmental use of our language on Earth is very deeply a part of my being. I do not apologize! My Earthly surroundings made me what I am today. I am proud!

"Therefore, all the formal tools of education, personal appearance and excellence in general are not as important to my new position as that which I found on the streets, and later living with a poor working family. I found an abundance of duty and loyalty on rainy and dark streets, and I found duty and loyalty sitting with a poor man dining on bread and beans. I am proud, Fellow Canines! I am proud I could learn duty and loyalty in these circumstances. I am very proud!

"Black Carolyn was proud while riding in a cart of rags on the streets. A little scared, cold and hungry puppy was proud, too! A lonely and friendless and frightened Black Labrador arrived in Canine Heaven with no Connections, and a very imperfect beginning. But she was proud!

"The homeless puppy, the street dog, the poor man's dog, stands before you now. I am accepting this fine position in Canine Heaven ... not only as a pretty face, a pretty coat and pretty fine intellect as I mentioned, but duty and loyalty as well, and I am MOST proud of that! Duty and loyalty, my Fellow Canines. Duty and loyalty.

"If I repeat myself, and I do, I am Carolyn! Something special! And I know I am! I am Carolyn! I am Carolyn!

"Call it arrogance if you must, but I call it proud. I am proud today. I will be proud tomorrow! I am Carolyn!

"Thank you, Your Greatness."

Carolyn's voice was soft, but still forceful and sincere as she finished. She hadn't really meant to give such a long recitation, and didn't know quite what she would say other than the acceptance of the position. She did not believe that she was expected to make a lengthy speech. Only a few short and cute phrases! If that was the case, it became impossible for Carolyn to honor any restrictions or expectations. Once started, Carolyn's speech took a theme from which she could not deviate. Duty and loyalty. She knew them both well!

Consequently, Carolyn made her case for Carolyn in a moving and splendid delivery! She wanted to be known as the Most Private Secretary in The Big Bone Palace, but more than that, she wanted to be known as Carolyn, the Black Labrador, who placed duty and loyalty above all else! Yes, Carolyn had sold herself ... not with quips, not with intellect, not with beauty, but only by being Carolyn, a near-perfect canine.

The applause was thunderous. Joyful canines were yapping and clapping, and standing on their seats to show a nice lady their approval and respect. Carolyn stood beside The Great Collie. She smiled as he said once again barely above a whisper:

"You are very welcome, my dear. You were great!"

Holy Joe and O'Casey moved forward on the stage to congratulate Carolyn. She knew she had done well. Reckoned maybe she was a "best speaker" without even trying to be! It was talking from the heart that made it a great speech, if indeed it was, and Carolyn, listening to the ovations, "reckoned" it was a great speech! The tears fell. It was Holy Joe who wiped them away. The same Holy Joe who had dried Carolyn's tears on another day in Fleecy Park. She remembered! He remembered!

The applause wore on as the canines paid tribute to Carolyn. They knew her now! She was great! And surviving in a wretched turbulent Earthly existence? Oh, The Great Collie had made the best choice alright! Carolyn! They kept on clapping until Wrangler stepped to the microphone and took control.

"Hey?" Wrangler called out, turning up the volume on the microphone as far as it would go. "Hey! Hey! Isn't anybody hungry yet? I'm starved! Carolyn appreciates your wonderful response to her appointment, and to her as a dutiful and loyal sister. We all thank you! We can sample the tasty treats on the picnic tables in a matter of minutes now! We will conclude this official meeting at this time. Brothers and Sisters, we give to you, The Great Collie!"

The Great Collie lost no time closing the meeting. He excused the Canine Council, and he excused and thanked all the canines. He excused those who had shared the stage with him, and then he took Carolyn's paw, and led her to the picnic tables.

Everything was informal and the canines dined at first one table then another. It was a happy group. So much camaraderie. So much chatting and congratulating the new appointees, and so much talk about Carolyn's speech. And there was a lively discussion going on about O'Casey's editorial as well.

The canines had read the editorial, and its contents were surprising along with O'Casey's style of presenting his opinions. And what about Little Ben? A sad thing, that was! How O'Casey must have suffered before he found his little brother. All of this made the residents see that O'Casey did have a lot of love in his heart after all! Maybe they hadn't known him well enough, and had judged him too harshly. And Lolita also. Well, maybe they had not judged Lolita harshly enough at times!

Most of the canines had not known. They had never heard of Lolita's grief and sorrow when she was young. It was obvious that Lolita loved taking care of the puppies, and it was obvious she did a fine job. But her arrogance and overbearing attitude was obvious, too. Now, maybe they could understand her a little better, and be more tolerant. A lot of them wanted to be, but this was almost impossible with Lolita's bossiness and outright testiness. A big aggravation to the residents, and Lolita was in character today! Loving to the puppies, impatient with the rest. What a lively topic Lolita was, though. And along with O'Casey and Carolyn, the canines had plenty to talk about!

Carolyn's speech was something, and just about everyone had something they just had to say!

"Would you believe that Carolyn had been a street dog?"

"No, and did you see how she talked about it with such grace?"

"Yes, I did! She overcame all those hardships, and she survived!"

And the talk, observations and analyzing went on and on while the Canine Heaven population dined on the scrumptious fare on the picnic tables. Hiro had done himself proud, and he had two big platters, beautifully arranged, of Chinese Noodles, too! The Great Collie smiled as he helped himself to a large serving. Delicious! That Hiro!

The old Black Dog had his family to himself now that the meeting was over. They enjoyed the food and chatting and just being together. Pasha had permission to join them for the picnic, and Noodles was there, too.

Noodles was a happy canine knowing he would be working with Bojangles. He was most happy, though, of being made a part of the Old Black Dog's family. It was unofficial, of course, but now he had friends that he could turn to in times of unrest. A real plus for him. He wasn't alone nor lonely any more, and today, here with a family, his family, he was happy! It was a fun day for all of them, and the Old Black Dog beamed!

Carolyn had chatted with the crowd, and accepted their congratulations for her promotion, and her speech as well. She answered the canine's questions about her life on Earth openly and honestly. It was only when Holy Joe came up to her with his paws full of scones that she found herself with little to say. She felt the tears again, but she smiled anyway, and said quietly:

"Hello again, Holy Joe."

"Carolyn, you have done yourself as proud as I am of you this day!"

"Thank you, Holy Joe," Carolyn said softly. "I never could, you know, with out your helping me and all."

"You would have in time, Carolyn. A smart canine like Carolyn does alright for Carolyn," Holy Joe smiled. "It's a big day for you, but you made it a big day for all of us, too! You know that, don't you?"

"Yes, I reckon I did pretty good." Carolyn laughed, intentionally reverting to her old way of speaking.

"I reckon you did, too!" he laughed along with her. "Yes, I reckon so!"

Holy Joe had been right about Carolyn all along. Ever since that day in Fleecy Park when she had shared a lonely and tortured past, he knew she just had to be something special! She, herself, was always saying it, too. And it certainly had turned out that way. How he had helped her, as she said, he was not sure, but if he had been of help, Holy Joe was happy and offered thanks. Carolyn WAS something special!

Little Ben was allowed to share the picnic with O'Casey, and O'Casey loved the idea so much, he introduced Little Ben to everyone!

"He's my brudder," Little Ben would say, and O'Casey would beam!

"Well, O'Casey," said Holy Joe. "So this is why you were so happy in Chapel yesterday."

"Yes, I guess it was," O'Casey told him. "I should have talked more about him before this, but there was a problem with Lolita. That's over now."

"Glad to hear it," smiled Holy Joe. "Good editorial, O'Casey, didn't sound like you at all."

"Well, I'll be back! You can count on that!" O'Casey laughed. "I just went a bit philosophical. I'll be back."

"I thought it was beautiful," Carolyn said as she and Lucy joined in the conversation. They were talking about O'Casey's editorial as well.

"It was beautiful!" Lucy agreed. "I almost cried when I read it."

"Thank you both," O'Casey was still smiling, and holding Little Ben's paw. "But Carolyn, you stole my heart with that fine speech. It was wonderful! I admit I was so proud of you, and proud that I was a friend, I cried! Well, it was almost crying."

"Thank you again, O'Casey. I wanted to tell before that I did cry over the beautiful phrases you used to show the caring and then your joy. Shame on you for not shedding real tears for me."

Carolyn was still teasing. She was still excited about everything! Everything!

"Your new position won't change you a bit, Carolyn," O'Casey was teasing, too. "You will still be telling us how special Carolyn is, and how pretty she is as well."

"You are forever a Hound Dog with a pair of good eyes!" Carolyn quipped.

The friends chatted and laughed and others joined them. Jetaway wanted to talk with Lucy, and Bojangles wanted a meeting with Carolyn. Since the two of them would be working at the Palace ... well, Bojangles thought SHE should get to know HIM.

"Why, Bojangles," Carolyn cooed. "I already know who you are. How nice you are, too, to seek me out in this huge, huge crowd. Now we won't be working as a team, you will be working for me, as well as the Great Collie and Wrangler. You remember that, OFFICE BOY, and you don't give me any trouble. If you do, I will personally pull your ears!"

Carolyn was smiling as she put both paws around Bojangles neck and ruffled his shaggy coat. Bojangles smiled back at Carolyn. He was liking her already!

Hildegard joined the group to offer her congratulations to Carolyn as well as to O'Casey. Drawing room etiquette demanded that she do so! After shaking O'Casey's paw, and telling him how the Little Ben matter should have been resolved more quickly, Hildegard turned her attention to Carolyn.

"My dear," she said, "you were very wonderful giving your speech with such little notice. I am sure you will do a fine job in your new position. We were all so proud that you could accept the facts of your heritage, and talk about them."

"Thank you, Hildegard," Carolyn answered in a measured tone. "But, I did not talk about my heritage. I spoke of my environment as it was on Earth, and furthermore, I have never spoken of my heritage except with Wrangler and Holy Joe. I never will, Hildegard. I don't need to! I am glad, though, you liked my speech, and do remember, if I maybe can be of service to you in my new position, it will be my pleasure!"

Carolyn smiled at Hildegard and offered her paw. The long-standing feud with "them Poodles" had been laid happily to rest. No need to declare about who won or lost. It simply didn't matter anymore!

"Yes, dear," Hildegard said, taking Carolyn's extended paw. "Thank you. I shall keep in touch."

"Carolyn, if you don't beat all! If you DON'T beat all!" Holy Joe told her after Hildegard had left them.

"Well, maybe I did put Hildegard in her place," Carolyn laughed. "But, you know, I didn't mean to. Not really. I think she understood, though. Hey, the party must be over. Everyone's heading for home."

It was true! The "party" was coming to an end, and it was time, for it had been a long, long day. Tiring and informative—suspenseful and satisfying—and just a great, great "together" day for both business and pleasure. All of the canines would remember this day as peaceful and joyful which their Canine Heaven was all about.

The Great Collie with Wrangler, and the Council members had already exited the Park. This was the signal! Lolita and her helpers guided the puppies out of the Park. The Seniors were returned to their Community, and the others got together with their particular groups. Racer and King called in their helpers to begin the cleanup. Buddy and Durkin packed their cameras, and were off to the newsroom. O'Casey would be very pleased with their work!

Tomorrow was another work day. But now, it was time to rest and reflect!

REST AND REFLECTION

Yes, it was time for rest. But for reflection, too! The excitement of today was still with the canines as they bedded down for the night. Each with a special thought and view of the event. Nevertheless, musn't forget prayers!

Lolita, with her helpers, had gathered the puppies along with Little Ben and Pasha, and guided them back to the Puppy Compound. The little fellows, so tired and excited, were not a big chore to get snuggled into bed. Lolita found herself tired as well. She excused her helpers, said good night, and rested.

"It was an excellent get-together," Lolita was thinking. "With all the announcements, appointments and changes, too, in Canine Heaven today, I am continuing as Director of the Puppy Community. Who else could do the fine job that I do everyday? Canis Major, thank you for looking out for the puppies. I thank you for looking out for me, too!"

Before she slept, Lolita thought of O'Casey, and the nice and kind way he had talked about her in his editorial. He had called her friend! Their problem having to do with Little Ben was a sore that had been healed. It had hurt them both.

"I never wanted to hurt O'Casey. It was just that I had to take care of my babies." Lolita told herself. "O'Casey was so imposing, but he's happy now. I had to do my job, though."

Lolita was proud of Carolyn for her good fortune, and she was pleased that Madeline, her former helper, had found a position that she liked.

"As manager of the "Brush and Clip" Salon, she should do fine. She did not enjoy working with the puppies which I don't understand. Maybe she didn't enjoy me either! Anyway, I shall call on her when the shop is in operation, extend my paw, and let her trim and clip my platinum coat. I shall smile, too! Now, how's that for being gracious and forgiving, Canis Major? A very, very, very good night to you!"

Carolyn said good night to Lucy, got herself ready for bed, but she couldn't drift off to sleep just yet. Too much had happened for an early rest. It was literally unbelievable! She would tell Canis Major all about it.

"Canis Major, I know I deserved the position of Most Private Secretary and I will be the best. I sure made a fine speech today, and I am proud of that. I am glad I stressed the duty and loyalty theme because that's what I truly believe. I never thought much about it on the streets with Millie, or living with the working people either. It was just the way I was, I reckon. But I am real proud that I could finally understand how I really was. I did survive, Canis Major, and I did pretty well all through it, didn't I?

"I think of those sweaters and ribbons that "them Poodles" wore, and how I wanted them, too. I bet the Poodles had sorrows of their own, though. And, I think Hildegard probably did also. I never knew a canine that didn't have a few troubles of some kind. I know I am going to be nice and helpful to Hildegard when I can, and I will mean it. I have good friends here, and I am happy most of the time. I am happy for this, and all the days yet to be.

"Canis Major, I still wonder why my Mama left us four puppies in the Shopping Mall. She wouldn't have willingly and I know that! She would be proud of me, I bet. I hope maybe she knows that I am proud of me, too. I hope she also knows that I am something special, and I always did know it! I am Carolyn! I am Carolyn, Canis Major! Thank you for looking out for me. I love you. A very good night!"

Carolyn's pretty coat shining, even in the dark, and her heart happy, this very special canine rested!

Bojangles was delighted that events of his first day in Canine Heaven went so well, and he was to spend the first night with Buster. Noodles had gotten permission to join them. Tomorrow, Bojangles would be assigned his quarters at The Big Bone Palace, and he was excited about that, and he was quite excited about starting his new job as an office boy for The Great Collie. This would all happen tomorrow.

Tonight, though, was for rest. But who could rest? Bojangles couldn't and neither could Buster and Noodles. Too much excitement for one day, and they needed to talk about it!

"We can talk for a little while, but remember, we have to say our prayers," Buster told his visitors. "There are a lot of canines trying to sleep. So you guys settle down. I am tired, and Bojangles, stop kicking!"

"Well, we are tired, too, Buster," Bojangles said. "And I'm not kicking a bit. That's my tail wagging. Because I know I will like it here."

"Yes, you will," Buster smiled. "I am glad you were given a good job like The Great Collie's office boy. That is nice for you. But I am content here as well, and I love singing in the choir, but the quartet is really my thing! Do you remember, Bojangles, how I did not serve your human family? I couldn't! I know they thought the sun rose and set in you. Gosh, but you were spoiled!"

"Yeah, I was spoiled. But, they did love you, too. A lot! And I am glad we can be better friends here. Aren't you glad also, Buster?"

"Yes, I am. And Noodles, what about your new position? Are you happy about it?" Buster wanted to know.

"Oh, I'm real pleased," Noodles answered. "I will be in and out of those places were Bojangles will be, so I'll see him every day. Do you guys know about what I'm really tickled?"

"Yes, we do!" Bojangles and Buster laughed together, "Yes, we do!"

"And, you are right!" Noodles said. "The old Black Dog decreed that I be a part of his family. Your family. And I like that a lot!"

"Will you guys try not to take more of the bed than you need? I am bigger than the both of you, and I need space to stretch out!" Buster grumbled. "Can we say our prayers now?"

"Okay," said Noodles. "I want to be first: Thank you, Canis Major. I had a real good day. You watched over me and gave me a family, and a nice new job.

"Thank you for helping me find Bojangles again. I have friends and family, and I am happy. Good night!"

"Well, that was sure a nice prayer, Noodles," Bojangles told him. "I don't think Canis Major knows me yet. I will try, though: Canis Major, my name is a pretty name, Bojangles. You will hear from me each evening, but first I want to tell you about me. I belong to the Old Black Dog's family, or Connections I guess they call it here. Anyway, I'm the new office boy to the Great Collie at The Big Bone Palace, but I guess he is already known to you. I don't think there will be much hard work. I don't like to work much, but I do like a lot of attention. I had that on Earth, and at the Briefing Center, too. I guess I am still spoiled. That's alright!

"I like Carolyn. She is so nice and pretty, too! Thank you for Noodles and Buster. Oh yes, and thank you for the Old Black Dog, Rover, Jetaway and that little puppy. I think they call him by the name of Pasha. Anyway, I love them all, and—"

"Heavenly Days, Bojangles!" Buster interrupted. "How much longer? You've run on and on. Now say good night! Canis Major knows a lot more about every canine than we might think!"

"He does?" asked Bojangles. "Why, I thought he didn't know me at all. I am just getting acquainted, Buster, and I don't want to be rude to Canis Major."

"You won't be! Now say good night!"

"Good night, Canis Major. I'm sorry some of us are so testy. I just wanted you to know about me, and how grateful I am for all the nice things that happened to me today, and—"

"Say good night, Bojangles." Buster urged. "You HAVE to say good night!"

"Good night, Canis Major, I want to talk more tomorrow night after I know more about my job, you see! I hope the Great Collie likes me, and—"

"Say GOOD NIGHT, Bojangles!"

"Good night again, Canis Major. You will hear from me soon. I promise! Do have a nice rest. Good night, to you!"

"Have you finished at last?" Buster asked. "Canis Major hears our prayers each evening, and they are not so very long. They don't need to be. I thought you'd never say good night!"

"Well, I—"

"Now you've already said good night so you just be quiet, and go to sleep. And, stop wagging your tail! I will be saying my prayers now, and then we are to go to sleep. Some of us have to be working tomorrow, you know! Noodles is already asleep."

"No, I'm not! I was listening to my friend's prayer." Noodles said. He put his paw on Bojangles' paw, and frowned at Buster.

"Oh, so now, I'm the heavy! I guess I'm not hosting this sleep-over." Buster smiled at Noodles quite firmly. "I note that you have said good night also, Noodles, and no more from your pal either! Now good night, you two!"

"Good night, Buster. We love you," two sleepy voices said.

"Thank you, Canis Major," Buster began his prayer. "This has been a happy day, and I'm happy that Bojangles will be with us from now on. I'm also happy that Noodles will spend more time with us as a family. Thank you for my singing with the quartet. I know what fine singing we did, too! Thanks again. And a very good night to you."

Buster noticed that both Bojangles and Noodles had quickly fallen asleep, and were curled tightly in two little black and white balls. Buster thought all of this was nice, and would go for ever with the family being together. A tired and happy canine laid his paw on his sleeping bed partners, kissed each head, and joined them in dreamland!

The old Black Dog and Rover, having said their good-byes, left Fleecy Park together. So much had happened on this day that was very satisfying, and the Old Senior wanted some company to talk about them, he told Rover. He invited Rover to spend the night as his guest. Now, Rover had spent the night before at the Senior Community when they were planning for Bojangles' arrival. Rover thought about the invitation. He must work the next day. But, he accepted it anyway! He needed some company, too. A few shared moments with his dear, dear friend would do just fine.

The song Rover had done had been so well received by The Great Collie, and His Greatness had shook Rover's paw. A great, great honor. He wanted to talk about it! The Old Black Dog wanted to talk about all of his "family". He was very proud of them! Maybe he and Rover wouldn't talk long before saying their prayers and taking their rest. Just a little conversation, though!

"You know, Rover, I was quite proud today."

"I know you were, Sir. I was, too! And of all of our family. We did get a lot of nice recognition."

"Your song was so good, Rover."

"Yes! I was pleased. Thank you! I'm an old Country Boy myself, you know."

"Yes! And there's no place like the country either. No one, whether animal or human, should ever be denied living in, or learning about the country."

"I agree with you, Sir. You need to know about country folks and their way of living and learning. You gain a lot in the country being so close to field and forest. You need to see the nature of all things. The seasons changing is not the same in the city. You need to experience this to know."

"Oh, you do need that. Yes, you do need that! City canines are not smart. They think they know all about everything, but they don't know that nature is real knowledge, and only nature."

"Yes, Sir, it is! Unless you dig a hole in the earth and feel the soil in your face, and feel it falling between your paws, you know very little. Knowledge is nature alright! And nature is knowledge!"

"Let's say our prayers now, Rover. We have a lot to thank Canis major for tonight."

"Yes, Sir, we will say our prayers," Rover said. "We both are tired. It was so kind of you to include Noodles. And I wanted to tell you so. I thought Bojangles was just alright! I do hope we see more of him than we do of Jetaway, don't you?"

"Yes, but they are not farm canines like we were, Rover. They have missed out on much learning. They are canines of their own Earthly environments. The same as we are! They just never had it as good as we did. We were lucky! They are our family, and we love all of our Connections including Noodles! Rover, why don't you say your prayer? Then I will say mine and we can rest."

"Thank you, Sir. Canis Major, thank you for "keeping" me today, and thank you for this wondrous place. I guess I am a "Country Boy", and I'm thankful I had the opportunity to be one. Thank you for my friend, the Old Black Dog. Canine Heaven is even more dear to me with his presence. Good night to you!"

"Thank you, Rover. Canis Major, you have made an old dog very proud today with your blessings. I do thank you! I thank you for my family, but mostly, I thank you for Rover. Good night."

The Old Black Dog and Rover settled themselves comfortably in bed and said good night to each other. They drifted off to sleep. Together! Just like they had done on Earth. And dreaming, too! Dreaming of watching the corn grow; of picking the blackberries; of gathering the cotton and hickory nuts. They were once again chasing the rabbits, squirrels and chickens; tending the cattle and other livestock. Dreaming of times long past!

They were never cold, never hungry, never abused and never lonely. Running free with the wind in the fields. Just being with one another. It was enough! More than enough! Rover snuggled close to the Old Black Dog as he slept. Yes, it had all been more than enough. And now they had earned Canine Heaven. It was enough! More than enough!

Jetaway talked with Lucy for awhile before leaving Fleecy Park. He wanted to start his new job as Librarian in a professional manner, he told Lucy. She advised him to ease into the position. He was thinking about this as he began the walk to his Community Residence.

Maybe Lucy was right. Maybe it was a good idea to slowly ease into a routine. Jetaway hadn't expected so great an honor, but he was pleased. He dusted his paws and brushed his coat as he prepared for bed. And he put together a plan, and made a decision, too!

Well, he didn't need much help from Lucy or anyone else. He would organize and manage the Library in his own way! And, with his own ideas and notions of how a Library should function. Jetaway was the Librarian now, and Jetaway was capable! Otherwise, why would Jetaway have been chosen by His Greatness? It was settled! Jetaway needed no outside help to manage the Library! He turned his thoughts to the day's events.

"The family was really together today," Jetaway told himself. "We were a united bunch. The Old Black Dog could not control his joy at seeing his family honored so many times. It was real nice, too!

"Bojangles is spoiled, and he won't do much except make others want to do things for him. That's alright, too. I remember when our human family made to do over me! I was spoiled as well. It took me awhile, here in Canine Heaven, to contribute all that I was capable of doing. Bojangles will learn in time.

"Rover and Buster did well in their singing. I was real proud of them. Pasha is cute, but I have nothing at all in common with him. The others do not either, but he is family so we mustn't forget about him. And speaking of forgetting! I will remember to hang on to my wings. I am Chief Librarian. Can't afford to goof off! So I won't!

"I won't fret so much either. Funny when I think of that Solar Eclipse now after all these years, and it is amusing how scary it was. Even the humans were scared. Of course I fretted! Who wouldn't with everything getting dark? And in the middle of the day? And then I was afraid of the thunder storms. Of course I was afraid. All canines are a sorry lot in a storm. It's funny now!

"I will be an excellent Librarian I have just decided. And I will choose a few assistants tomorrow, too. I am exhausted so will say my prayers and get some sleep. Tomorrow will be busy!"

Jetaway had made his plans, and all was right. He knew it!

"Canis Major," Jetaway began. "What I was going to tell you, you know. You were good to me today, and I will not disappoint anyone in my duty as a very good Librarian. Watch over the family, and do help us to be more tolerant and kind to each other. We're pretty good, but we can do better. Thank you."

Jetaway was ready after his prayers to rest. He felt good. He made himself comfortable, opened and shut his eyes. Opened and shut his eyes a time or two and then—.

Freddie and Fresca walked to their Community together, and prepared themselves for bed without saying much. It was not long, though, before Freddie's frustration had to be recognized!

"Well, I was aggravated, Fresca! It was almost insulting! That crowd only wanted to hear that silly "Toot, toot" number. We didn't get to do our others that we had rehearsed so well. I liked those songs, too! That dumb "Toot!""

"Yes," answered Fresca. "But it was a fun thing for the canines, and being in a party mood, too, they went a mite wild. They would never behave in Chapel like that. But what the heck! This was a festive day, Freddie."

"I know you are right! "Toot, toot" is a lively number, and the canines do have fun with it. I won't be grouchy."

Fresca knew Freddie quite well, and she didn't, for a moment, believe that Freddie's grouchiness was over. No, it wouldn't be reconciled before Freddie said her prayers and told Canis Major.

Fresca, though, snuggled into bed. Smiled good night to Freddie. Said her prayers, and was soon sleeping. Fresca was never upset enough about anything to lose sleep over! Freddie was a little different when meeting challenges, and, like Jetaway, she fretted so much more than she should at times!

In the first place, Freddie was delighted that His Greatness had chosen her as the organist for the Chapel. It was extra duty that she could handle, and still have time for the quartet. A chorus out of control was what worried her. The chorus wasn't really all that bad, but it needed more time than even Gertrude had found. Working with those Bulldogs, and their bass voices would be a chore, and then, there was Hildegard, the busybody French Poodle, who was assigned to the Chapel. How could she keep Hildegard in line, and still improve the chorus?

"Well, I will!" vowed Freddie. "If I am in charge, I will be in charge! And I will have a talk the first thing tomorrow morning, with both Holy Joe and Hildegard! That settles that! I am going to say my prayers and lie down. It has been a long busy day. Canis Major thank you for helping me today. And I will do fine in all my new duties. And perhaps I am vain, but if any resident canine here knows more about music, I would like to know who it is! I am sad that I am testy tonight. I don't mean to be. Please forgive me! Maybe I want to talk about my time on Earth tonight for a little while.

"I get to thinking sometimes of the nice life I had, you know. Anyway I do want to tell you about my friend, Callie, a Golden Retriever. We had a cat, Tiger. Tiger was big and yellow. Not a real friend to Callie and me. But cats never are to canines. They just share an uneasy peace! Callie and I did get along with Tiger, though, and if there is a Feline Heaven, I know that Tiger is there. She served our Mistress real well. Just as I did, and just as I know that Callie continues to do.

"I wish Callie and my Mistress knew about Canine Heaven, and how wonderful being here is. Callie will join me one day, and together we can share all our memories. All of them, Canis Major! We can snuggle into bed as we did so long ago, and be together. Earth was a good life, and happy times, and I remember how joyful our Mistress made it for us everyday! Maybe we were not perfect. I don't think our Mistress intended that we be. So we served! And that's why I am here. Waiting for Callie!

"I am not sad anymore after talking with you, Canis Major. It was really a good coming together today. All those happy, smiling faces! Well, I won't be grouchy! I can rest now. Thank you!"

Freddie had unburdened herself. She felt so much better since she had told Canis Major all about her aggravations. The excitement of the day had been one big "bang", and she had been one of an exciting group of honorees, too! A big honor to be sure, but a big challenge, as well. Freddie brushed her coat, and smiled at the sleeping Fresca.

Holy Joe had enjoyed the picnic and all the festivities at Fleecy Park on this day. He knew most of the appointments already so there were only a few surprises. And he had been pretty certain that Carolyn would be chosen Most Private Secretary. When that happened, Holy Joe was almost as pleased as she. He had approved of the other honorees, too, and thought there was some mighty fine talent in Canine Heaven. Holy Joe was musing about this when he saw that O'Casey had flopped down on his bed in such a hurry and pretended to already be asleep! Their beds were close together in the Community where they resided so before bedding down himself, he wanted to know O'Casey's opinion of the day's events.

"Alright, O'Casey," Holy Joe said. "I know you're not asleep. I bet you're pretty tired, though. Were you working all of last night?"

"Yep! Most of it anyway. I slept at my desk for awhile. I had to be at the Landing Site at noon. You know to take pictures of Bojangles, that new Palace employee. He is spoiled, but likable. Did you meet him?"

"Just for a moment. He was a happy, happy fellow. Nice family, too. And he IS spoiled! He will be fine, though. I thought His Greatness made a valuable, and pleasing address. The Science Laboratory is a wonderful idea. And with enough research, I think it will be an excellent tool to developing a limited communication with Earth, if not a desired all-out contact. What say you?"

"Oh, I say yes!" O'Casey answered. "That laboratory will produce. It will take time, but it will be successful! You know that Great Dane, Roberto, has to be a good choice to head this project from what I hear. Some friends of his say he is working on a kind of instrument in his spare time. Something electronic, they said. He had $E=MC^2$ on his briefcase when he arrived here two months ago. I don't know him, do you?"

"No, I hadn't even seen him before. Until today, that is. It will be very interesting to watch his progress. You know, O'Casey, I was pleased for Carolyn."

"Me, too! she deserves this chance. Carolyn's appointment was the only one I did not know. I already knew all the others as I had been directed to privately handle the matter of getting an item in the Canine Weekly.

And that's one of the reasons I am exhausted. The other is printing those flyers on such short notice," O'Casey yawned. "I had Buddy and Durkin help with the flyers, but the announcements, I did alone as I had been instructed."

"I can see why you are tired," said Holy Joe. "Maybe I'm keeping you from your rest. I'll say good night."

"Cut the nonsense, Holy Joe! I need to talk more than you do tonight. And, you know it, don't you?"

"Well, I do know we both like talking over things after one of these events," Holy Joe smiled at O'Casey and continued. "There were few surprises in the appointments, and only a few in the messages. I knew them all, too."

"You did?" O'Casey asked surprised. "I had those papers under lock and key in my office! Did you sneak around there and read them when I was getting a few winks at my desk?"

"No, of course not!" Holy Joe told him. "I just used that old process of elimination method, that's all. I even used it in Carolyn's case. Who else is as deserving as she is? And her speech was magnificent, too. Do you know she told Wrangler that she couldn't make a speech? I laughed about that."

"Yes, I did, too," said O'Casey. "I thought Carolyn was great! But getting back to how you knew so much. I should have known that any canine as intelligent as yourself, could arrive at some pretty accurate conclusions. But tell me, did you learn how to analyze, deduce and solve problems in the Commune with those Hippies?"

"Absolutely!" Holy Joe answered. "I had an education in the Commune that I imagine was unparalleled. I do hope it remains the same today."

"It does!" said O'Casey. "It does! And with you and Wrangler both working on the Great Charter, I bet that code will be broken someday soon. Wrangler is intelligent and very able. Like you are, I think."

"Well, O'Casey, I bet when some one deciphers that code, you will be in on it, too! With your super intellect, I don't think you should applaud me and Wrangler too highly," Holy Joe teased.

"Thank you! Holy Joe, tell me something before I say my prayers. What do you really think of my editorial? And, were you delighted with Little Ben?"

"Your editorial was one fine piece of journalism, O'Casey. Your heart and soul was evident throughout. I was relieved for I had been worried about a few things having to do with you. You know, we all hear different music, and therefore, we march to different drummers. That is why we need to love and respect others for what they are. Not for what we would like them to be. I learned that in the Commune, too! I am glad the problem with Lolita was solved. We can all understand Lolita better. I like her! And Little Ben? He is simply delightful! Both of you are indeed fortunate. We must say our prayers now so you can rest. This was your day also, O'Casey! You "done" good!"

"Thank you again, Holy Joe. You do make words flow like music. I guess it is a gift from the Commune as well. Am I right?" O'Casey yawned again.

"Well, as a matter of fact, we were always learning something. We had some passionate speakers in the Commune who were law students. They loved to hear themselves argue. They were eloquent!" Holy Joe told him. "It was always such an honor to be associated with them. I am grateful, but enough of that. Would you please say your prayers. I want to hear them on this special day. Then I will say mine."

"Canis Major," O'Casey began. "You have heard me, and you have helped me. I thank you! Good night, Canis Major."

"That's it?" Holy Joe asked. He was surprised.

"That's it!" answered O'Casey.

Holy Joe thought about the prayer, but only for a moment. He understood. O'Casey had made a sincere and beautiful declaration of gratitude. No need for him to express himself in more detail, and just as his editorial had so eloquently touched many hearts on this day, O'Casey's short prayer had had a similar effect. Beautiful!

"Canis Major," Holy Joe said as he began his own nightly prayer. "Today, you have served us, and we have served each other. Many wonderful things happened here today. And many wonderful things will happen tomorrow and all of the tomorrows to come! How fortunate we are! Good night, Canis Major."

Holy Joe, seeing the huge frame of O'Casey already deep in sleep, smiled to himself as he prepared for bed.

"This is good!" Holy Joe was quietly saying. "This is very good. A very good night to you, O'Casey. You came a long, long way to get here today, but your trip was so worthwhile! Every canine knows you do have a heart. A generous and loving heart. You brought it for us all to see today. Have a good rest, my friend. You earned it!"

O'Casey, wrestling with Little Ben in his dreams, heard not a word spoken by Holy Joe. And climbing into his own bed, Holy Joe was happy. Soon he found he was chasing the cats and barking at the rabbits back in the Commune as he dreamed, too!

Racer and King, of course, were the last to leave Fleecy Park. After going through a massive clean-up of the Park and environs, they excused their helpers, and headed for their Community to rest. Much needed rest, too! Racer and King, like O'Casey, were just "beat".

Yes, the nocturnal duty had taken a big toll, but their satisfaction had a big feeling of success as well. And it was such a good feeling, they both had a laugh about it. The two friends were too tired to argue, and laughter was a best defense. When King mentioned the benefits of laughter in their particular situation, they laughed about that along with everything else!

At their Community Residence, Racer and King removed their collars and began to brush each other. That brushing sure felt good! So relaxing! Maybe say prayers now. Then sleep! Sleep! What a beautiful word! As they brushed, Racer and King began to talk. It was decided that they were too wound-up to go down into the covers right away. Release is what they needed!

"Racer, I liked O'Casey's editorial so much," King said. "I never would've thought he had such kind words for any canine."

"Yes," answered Racer. "He surprised a bunch of us. I never would've believed it either, unless I read it myself."

"Carolyn's speech was sure nice. I am glad for her, too. You know, being a street-dog probably wasn't easy. I'm just happy for her."

"Well, I'll tell you something I am pretty pleased about, along with being happy for Carolyn, of course. And that is the way everything came together as it was supposed to for this event. The only major crisis was when Lolita went after Poncho. That was aggravating. He is a nice fellow, Poncho is. You know, King, some of those puppies are bigger than most of the Toy Canines, and they have to defer to the puppies, too, the same as we all do. Strange, isn't it? I did get a kick out of Hildegard, you know. What a busy Poodle she is!"

"I did, too. Hildegard is one of a kind alright. I didn't mean to be disrespectful, but we were busy. Just no time to explain to her that we did not need her expertise as she calls a real case of her being a busybody! Well, I think I'll say my prayers and turn in. Are you ready to call it a day?"

"I've been ready since last night," laughed Racer. "You go ahead and pray in private, King, and I will as well."

Racer and King curled themselves in their beds. They each said short private prayers, and fell quickly asleep.

King expressed his thanks to Canis Major in his prayer, and asked for the Deity's help in future endeavors. King was a fine canine well-liked, and very much at peace with himself. Happy and contented, this Rottweiler was, too!

King had served a kind Master when his military duty with Napoleon's army was finished. King had not enjoyed his chores of rounding-up prisoners of war and guarding the army. He was thankful when those days were over. Afterwards, he led an active, but peaceful, existence in a village in Germany. His new Master was a Civil Engineer, and King, always at his Master's side, watched a skilled Master lay out cities and plan roads and bridges. King enjoyed building canals most of all, and a lot of years later, he designed and built the popular swimming pond at Fleecy Park which happened to be in Canine Heaven! Being so well qualified, for King to be given the position of Maintenance Manager and Supervising Engineer was really no surprise. This was Canine Heaven. They wanted the best. They got the best!

Racer's prayer was short, too. What was there to ask for? He was contented and happy in Canine Heaven, and he was satisfied with his position. Racer and King were alike in these matters. They worked well as a team since their jobs overlapped in many ways. The two were good friends, and each respected other views and suggestions in their jobs of environment, conservation or planning considerations. His Greatness was most pleased.

Racer was like King in another way, too. He had acquired a real Master only after a more public duty. That Duty was Greyhound Racing! Fun at first, as Racer was young and in fine shape. He grew to realize that racing was not an enviable calling. It was a cruel sport with lots

of pain. Racer knew he could not win and perform con-
tinually as was expected of Greyhounds. He was glad to
finally be free of it.

Racer, adopted by a Forest Ranger, spent his days
among the trees in the National Parks. He worked for the
good of the environment, and helped to make the Parks a
place of refuge for all of those who would seek the comfort. Man or beast! Racer often thought how much more
satisfying his new job was than a silly chase involving a
Mechanical Rabbit around an oval track!

Almost as a bonus for his new life, Racer had had
the opportunity to serve a kind and devoted Master. His
own devotion had earned him Canine Heaven. A lot to
be thankful for. Nothing to ask of Canis Major! As Director of Fleecy Park, Racer's work could continue. All
that he had learned in the forests and National Parks would
now benefit Fleecy Park. It was good. Very good!

Hildegard had been one of the last to leave Fleecy
Park after the picnic. She had not joined the others returning to the Senior Community as she did not view herself as a Senior. Heavens, she was just too active and
connected to retire in an atmosphere of peaceful recollec-
tions! There was so much to do and to accomplish even
in one's afterlife. Hildegard told herself this over and
over.

Walking toward the Senior Community after re-
alizing there was no one left to talk with, Hildegard
thought of her experiences on Earth, and how valuable
these collective assets were to Canine Heaven, if only
The Great Collie would see! There were far too many
Commoners among the residents, and Hildegard using her

vast store of culture, learned in an elite society, could be of great service. So many would benefit. Well, perhaps most of the canines were happy enough with limited experience in such affairs. Hildegard decided it probably was the reason why so few reached out, and received personal cultivation. It was very strange!

When Hildegard arrived at her residence, she looked to see who might enjoy discussing the day's events before bedding down. Most had already settled in, but a few pretended to be asleep! Only Marsha, an Afghan, greeted Hildegard. Marsha was pretty, and almost as fastidious in her grooming. Marsha only tolerated Hildegard for this shared vainness.

"You are late, Hildegard. I wondered if you were doing the new job yet."

"Oh, no, dear," answered Hildegard. "I was only thinking of the changes to be made with the choir, and other activities, too. I imagine Freddie has a host of ideas, and I will assist her."

"I know you will. I expect Freddie to do an excellent job. She is really very talented."

"Of course, she is, dear! There are things she will need to learn. Arranging different voices for the best effect is something that I know a lot about. I saw so many musical events of all kinds with my Mistress. I went all over the world to concerts, recitals, and operas," Hildegard gushed. "Yes, I can help Freddie, and I expect to give Holy Joe advice, too. He is good with his sermons, but maybe added emphasis on certain grammatical terms, and Holy Joe could be a great orator. I am sure I can help him!"

Hildegard saw that Marsha was yawning daintily, but Hildegard wanted one more item covered before she, herself, retired.

"Marsha, the "Brush and Clip Salon" is a great idea, I think. Many canines will benefit from such a service. What do you think?"

"It is a good idea," Marsha agreed. "You know, Lolita and I, being of the same breed, have helped each other all along with our grooming. One could say we both are rather vain!"

"Oh, don't worry about being vain, dear. It's quite alright! Goodness, if I didn't have my own personal stylist, I can't imagine what I'd look like. As I traveled with my Mistress, you know, I had my own private groomer along. I have a silly little Whippet, Francine, a clerk at the Palace, who loves combing and clipping my coat. She does an excellent job, don't you think?"

"Oh, yes, I do, Hildegard. You always look like you just stepped out of a fine salon!" Marsha yawned again. "I had a personal groomer also."

"Oh, you did, dear? That's very interesting! I don't know where Francine learned her trade, but she sure gets a puff in the right place! I will give a try at the new salon. If I'm not really pleased, then Francine said she would continue to "do" me."

"That's nice! I am tired so I will say good night, Hildegard. Have a good rest. I expect you will be plenty busy tomorrow as usual."

"Good night, dear. Yes, I am sure it will be a busy day," Hildegard smiled. "I have good vibes about my assignment at the Chapel, and I know Holy Joe is delighted as well!"

As Hildegard prepared for her rest, she noticed that Marsha was asleep.

"Marsha could be of more help to me in organizing Canine Heaven's societal matters if she chose. Some Seniors are just content to "retire" in more ways than one. I declare, Marsha. I am glad I'm not one of your lazy sort!" Hildegard said as she watched Marsha sleeping. "No concern for the Arts."

Hildegard found herself a bit tired also, but first she must talk to Canis Major. Lots to tell him!

"Dear, dear Canis Major," Hildegard said. "Your great light shines on the cultured and the uncultured alike. Do help those who need your help in that regard! We could have a splendid slate of social activities if this happened. Maybe one day it will!

"Us French Poodles have learned our lessons well, and that is why we are a cut above the usual canines who served in the usual way. Our service had such class. Real class. But you know that, Canis Major, as well as I. With assistance from you, we can achieve a fine, elegant plateau of culture with an exquisite existence for all canines.

"Thank you, Canis Major, for my new assignment at the Chapel. I shall perform superbly as always! A very, very good night to you."

Well, this was just Hildegard being Hildegard, and full of ideas. And full of herself, too! She lay on her bed, a paw protecting the huge puff of neatly trimmed hair on her head. She fluffed her leg puffs, and stretched her legs in a graceful pose. Then, smiling and satisfied, Hildegard slept.

The Great Collie, Wrangler, and a few Whippet aides had gathered in the office of His Greatness to go over the day's events. This was customary when an official affair had taken place. It was over in a little while as everyone was yawning!

After recording the reports of the Security Whippets, the aides were excused. Security had checked every Community as they did each evening, and a written report showed all was quiet in Canine Heaven. The Great Collie smiled and reckoned it could be expected this night since all the canines were tired from the day's festivities. His Greatness was tired also. But there was an item or two that he wanted to discuss with Wrangler.

"Well, Wrangler," The Great Collie said when they were alone. "It was ONE interesting day, don't you think? And, it has been quite an interesting week. We both need some rest."

"Yes, Sir, it was interesting. And, as you said, we were certainly busy in a lot of things," Wrangler replied. "I look forward to another week of hectic activity. We have lots to do with many changes to process."

"Oh, yes, we are looking at a busy, busy time, that's for sure! I think we will tackle Science and Research first as our number one project. Make a note to summon Roberto to the Palace tomorrow afternoon. We will summon King tomorrow morning and go over plans for a suitable structure. It is important we begin immediately. Are you with me on this, Wrangler? Following me alright?"

"Yes, Sir, I am," said Wrangler. "I think we should start with Roberto and find out his initial ideas, and go on from that point. After researching his file, I understand he was learning all the time as his Master seldom left his scientific projects for any reason. It seems, Roberto's Master loved science, and it was passed to Roberto. He is an excellent choice."

"Yes, that is very true, Wrangler," The Great Collie told him. "Roberto is well qualified. He hasn't been here in Canine Heaven long. He will be current on procedures in electronics. I am of the notion that this project will be a great success in time."

"The project will succeed, and I am sure of that! Sir, we do have Roberto scheduled for a meeting at the Palace. That's in the afternoon. He will brief his assistant himself. We have King on call for early morning. Do you find my memo and suggestions satisfactory?"

Wrangler was writing feverishly on his clipboard as he waited for a reply from The Great Collie. He was ready to make any changes requested. Or to add to his memos! Or to subtract! Wrangler was a wonder, and like The Great Collie had said in his tribute earlier today about Wrangler, "I don't think Canine Heaven could get along without him."

"Those ideas are good, Wrangler. I am satisfied. You are a great help! Do you think the changes that we made today will work out? I know we can make further changes if necessary, but I am feeling pretty good about today. What about you?"

"Well, Sir, I am feeling real good about Carolyn. She will be a dedicated Most Private Secretary. I thought her speech was superb!"

"You know, Wrangler, Carolyn spoke from her heart. It took an outstanding canine to carry the theme of duty and loyalty, and stress it with such conviction! Yes, Carolyn will do fine. It will never get dull in the Palace with Carolyn around!" laughed His Greatness. "And, Wrangler, I was hoping she could see her pretty coral shell desk today but decided she had had enough excitement. She will see it tomorrow. Wrangler, please tell me what do you think of my Office Boy, Bojangles?"

"I think he is a spoiled canine. He is lazy, too!" Wrangler teased. "But, I like him. He's going to work all sides of the equation, though, and you will, I suspect, wind up doing his work."

"You are funny, Wrangler, but, alas you are also right, and I'm ready! It will be fun. You know, something quite different from the usual. Bojangles is from a nice family, and I am glad that Jetaway will head the Library. I liked him so much when he came to the Palace yesterday. We had a nice talk after he calmed down. He was worried about that Press Pigeon News Release. I spoke to O'Casey. It won't happen again!"

"No, Sir, it won't be repeated! The situation will be taken care of," said Wrangler. "O'Casey told me so today."

"Good! Make a note to follow up! I liked Rover's Country Boy song. How about you, Wrangler? Sure brought a lot of memories back for me."

"Rover did a good job, and he loved shaking paws with you. That was a very thoughtful gesture, Your Greatness!"

"Well, I meant it!" said The Great Collie. "We are tired, but, the events of the day, you know, I want to talk a little longer about some of them. That is, if you're not too tired."

"Sir, I'm enjoying our chat."

"Thank you, Wrangler. O'Casey wrote a fine editorial, didn't he? Very kind words were said for Lolita. They have reached an understanding. And that is good! I wonder how Holy Joe and Freddie will handle Hildegard."

"Very gingerly," laughed Wrangler. "O'Casey spoke his heart and his words reflected that feeling, too. It's like he said, you just never know about us, what loads we carry, what makes us the canines that we are. It's all very interesting, Your Greatness. We honestly don't know one another, do we?"

"No, we don't, Wrangler. Our files, you know, only tell a little about us. The real story is inside the canine."

"Yes, Sir, our real story is deeply buried within each of us. Maybe it is shared. Maybe not! Personally, I have not spoken much of my time on Earth. I don't recall you speaking of your days either, Your Greatness."

"Oh, I do think of my days on Earth a lot. Just as you must think of those times, too, Wrangler. Perhaps one day, my friend, we shall confide in one another. We spend so much time together, you know. Until then, have a peaceful rest. Good night, Wrangler. You are excused." The Great Collie said slowly.

He was thinking Wrangler might want to deal with his own story and needs, instead of always solving problems for others. Funny, but he had never thought about

Wrangler that way! Maybe after a good rest, he could think about it tomorrow.

The Great Collie wondered, though, why Wrangler's late night conversation had interested him so much. Was there something bothering his most important associate, and closest of all canines? Yes, he would look into this tomorrow!

His Greatness smiled, and Wrangler prepared to depart gathering his notes and papers.

"Thank you, Sir. Good night, we will both have a good rest," said Wrangler. "At least, we will try!"

The Great Collie smiled again as he took Wrangler's outstretched paw and held it warmly. These two were close!

"A fine Whippet, Wrangler is." His Greatness said when Wrangler had gone.

He summoned Blue, his valet, to see that his coat was brushed, and to prepare his bed.

Wrangler planned to say his prayers as he walked to his quarters. Pausing, though, when he approached the one-way communication device, he saw its giant screen flashing. This was the Briefing Center advising that newcomers would be arriving in Canine Heaven. Wrangler noted the message and dates, and still writing on his clipboard, he read the first few names:

Sam Dog, Cocker Spaniel
Callie, Golden Retriever
Chelsea, Shetland Sheep Dog
Tiger, Terrier
Grits, Labrador Retriever

Asta, Terrier
Roland, Irish Wolfhound
Josephine, Afghan Hound
Baby Doll, Toy Poodle

"They keep coming, and they will be welcome in Canine Heaven," said Wrangler almost reverently. He recorded the data on each one before moving on.

Briskly walking down the shiny hall of polished shells, Wrangler began his nightly prayer. This night, though, he was especially introspective, and did not know why. He needed to talk!

"Canis Major, I am so much a part of the Palace that many of the residents probably never think that I had a life on Earth, too. But, you and I know it! Don't we? They would be surprised!

"My service is to the residents and their needs. Or to The Great Collie. I will tell my story, though. I hope the proper time will come. Right now, I do have so much to do, and I will keep on serving with a happy and grateful face and heart! I am who I am, Canis Major!

"The past is gone, Canis Major, and can not hurt any canine again. And me? Never! Ever again! The past must rest! With your help, it WILL rest, and I do thank you, Canis Major.

"Thank you for a productive day. We all benefited. A pleasant good night." Wrangler had reached his quarters, and seeing the Whippet aides still not abed, but talking over the events of a day that Wrangler couldn't forget anymore than they could. He joined them!

The Great Collie dismissed Blue and made himself comfortable in his bed.

He looked upward to Sirius, the Dog Star, as he said his prayer:

"Canis Major, your blessings are so greatly appreciated this fine and productive day!

"Officially speaking for the whole wonderful population of Canine Heaven, I, The Great Collie, thank you. A very good night."

My Winter Has Come

Oh, my days were so full,
And time passed on wings.
My duties were never done
But there was joy in knowing-
I would always be showing
A devotion to many things-
Many, many things!
Now all too soon
Before the flowers again bloom,
My winter has come.
But once more I am young
And I race through the fields,
I jump and I leap and I bound!
As I work and I play and I love-
My song of life not yet sung.
Now, my winter is come-
My winter is here!
Yes, I know that all too soon-
Ere the flowers again bloom,
My winter has come.